GRITTITUDE

CHOOSE YOUR OWN LIFE STORY

KAY WOODBURN
JACQUI FLAVELL

Disclaimer - No Medical Advice

The information in this book, whether provided in hardcopy or digitally (together 'Material') is for general information purposes and nothing contained in it is, or is intended to be construed as medical advice. It does not take into account your individual health, medical, physical or emotional situation or needs. It is not a substitute for medical attention, treatment, examination, advice, treatment of existing conditions or diagnosis and is not intended to provide a clinical diagnosis nor take the place of proper medical advice from a fully qualified medical practitioner. You should, before you act or use any of this information, consider the appropriateness of this information having regard to your own personal situation and needs. You are responsible for consulting a suitable medical professional before using any of the information or materials contained in my Material or accessed through my website, before trying any treatment or taking any course of action that may directly or indirectly affect your health or well being.

Copyright © 2022 by Kay Woodburn & Jacqui Flavell

ISBN13 Paperback: 978-1-915771-02-5

ISBN13 Hardback: 978-1-915771-03-2

All rights reserved.

No part of this book may be reproduced in any form or by any electronic or mechanical means, including information storage and retrieval systems, without written permission from the author, except for the use of brief quotations in a book review.

CONTENTS

Preface   9
Praise for Kay Woodburn, Jacqui Flavell and Grittitude   11
Introduction   17
Kay Woodburn

Introduction   25
Jacqui Flavell

How To Use This Book   31

PART 1
THE ADVENTURE STARTS HERE

1. Grittitude   35
2. The Atlas   51
3. Don't Read This Chapter   61
4. Cold, Hard Truths   78
5. Beyond The Bullshit   95
6. Here's The Thing   113
7. One Day You'll Die   121

PART 2
THE MESSY BIT IN THE MIDDLE

8. Feels Like Heaven   125
9. Dreams, Goals and Buckets   139
10. Have You Got Crabs?   153
11. Cagoules, Sunscreen, And Bobble Hats   164
12. Twenty Seconds   177
13. Say YES To The Mess   194
14. The Confidence Myth   200

PART 3
DISCOVERING A NEW PATH

15.	The Broken Compass	211
16.	A 2nd Cup Of Tea	215
17.	The Spirit Level	224
18.	You believe you can choose your own life story	231
	Acknowledgements	233
	Kay Woodburn	237
	Jacqui Flavell	239
	Notes	241

DEDICATION

For Stewart
You promised to lift me up; thank you for keeping your promise.

For Jade and Cameron
The fish really did cross the road.

DEDICATION

For Malcolm
I love the story we have created together.
Thanks for making my spirits rise.

For Martha, Madeleine and Jude
I wish you lives filled with love, happiness and grittitude.

PREFACE

gritt·i·tude

[ˈgrɪtatɪtjuːd]

NOUN

comprising *grit* (courage and determination) and *attitude* (an enduring way of thinking, feeling or behaving towards something):

'S/he has grittitude towards all events faced in life, work and sport.'

synonyms: determination, passion, boldness, bravery, courage, discipline, guts, intrepidity, spunk, adventurousness, perseverance, power of mind

PRAISE FOR KAY WOODBURN, JACQUI FLAVELL AND GRITTITUDE

> "Kay has a clear and enthusiastic voice as a coach, both because of her passionate curiosity about human potential and her courage in applying principles to her lived experience"

DARYLL SCOTT – PSYCHOLOGICAL PERFORMANCE COACH, NLP EXPERT AND AUTHOR

> "Kay is a standout person and a highly effective coach. She always takes the time to get to know you as a person and then gets the best out of you and your performance"

LEON TAYLOR - BBC COMMENTATOR AND OLYMPIC MEDALLIST

> "Jacqui helps me to question the negative stories I tell myself. She helps me acknowledge all the evidence that challenges my beliefs. Since working with her I have become more confident and have more self-belief"
>
> NAIMA BEN-MOUSSA – 'THE LADY IN RED', FOUNDER AND CEO, REBUILDING LIVES UK – SUPPORTING SURVIVORS OF DOMESTIC ABUSE

> "Kay has transformed my outlook on the world. We all tell ourselves stories about what is happening around us and to us, some positive but many negative. Now I have a greater understanding of how these stories come about and how they can be interpreted and changed to achieve my goals at work and in life"
>
> MARK THOMPSON - EDITOR, NATIONAL WORLD PUBLISHING

> "This book will open your eyes to how you can be your own worst enemy. With great insight and individual case studies, it brings the learning to life. You will gain huge understanding of how to take control and change your story - how to unleash your own personal grittitude"
>
> DEE FAGG – CHIEF DOCUMENT ARCHITECT, 3 DOC SOLUTIONS

> "Jacqui is an exceptional coach, mentor and facilitator. She always knows just the right questions to ask that generate new thinking, new possibilities and choice for her clients"
>
> GRANT ALDRED – DIRECTOR, LEAD COACH INSPIRE LTD., ACC, CIPD

> "Kay's support has been instrumental in helping me get rid of my anxiety and clear my mind from years of negative thoughts and self-criticism. It's truly amazing!"
>
> CATH JESSE - PRODUCT INNOVATION CONSULTANT

> "Jacqui's coaching prowess astonishes people, me included. Within a few questions, she unearths the 'real problem' instead of the perceived problem they come to the session with"
>
> ALAYNE KELLY - MANAGING DIRECTOR, A LANE FORWARD

> "Jacqui is amazing! She asks the questions needed to really unravel how I was thinking negatively, why I thought that way and how I could re-frame certain feelings and experiences. I came away feeling excited about how to start and keep challenging my negative thoughts - and I can honestly say it made a massive difference in how I approach things"
>
> DANIELLE FOTHERINGHAM

> "Kay is inspiring, motivational, and thought-provoking. I am always in awe of Kay's ability to listen whilst creating an arena of thought and self-reflection, producing true grit, not to mention having a lot of fun along the way! Truly inspirational"
>
> JONATHAN DEAN - HEAD OF BUSINESS IMPROVEMENT

> "Kay is amazing. She has coached me through some really hard times. My life has become more positive, and she has helped me change the way I think. Eternally grateful!"
>
> FRANCESCA DAVIS - HEAD OF TALENT, PETS AT HOME

> "I worked with Jacqui at a very challenging time in my life. I was low in confidence and my body image was poor. A year on, my thoughts and outlook have been transformed for the better. I'm kinder to myself, work with myself rather than against and finally have the confidence to live boldly! I'm the happiest and most fulfilled I have ever been and am excited about life and all the possibilities that lie ahead"
>
> JO WALTON - WILD SWIMMER AND CANCER SURVIVOR

> "Kay's knowledge is mind-blowing. I learn more every session and leave feeling like a better person, more positive, more confident, more relaxed, more mentally prepared and so much more"
>
> JOEL RIZZI - PROFESSIONAL ATHLETE

> "Jacqui is a truly excellent coach who asks the relevant powerful questions, teasing the curiosity to find the answer. It is a symbiotic relationship where one cannot be successful without the other"
>
> CECILIA WILDE - LEADER, BUSINESS OPERATIONS, CISCO INTERNATIONAL LTD

INTRODUCTION

KAY WOODBURN

This is the bit where I'm supposed to convince you to keep this book in your hands and give you all the reasons you should read it. Look, I'm going to start as I mean to go on—with complete and utter honesty.

I've never been a fan of following the 'normal' route, the 'traditional' path, or doing what I'm 'supposed' to do. On the rare occasions I have followed the status quo, at best it's been a mind-numbingly boring experience and at worst it's been completely suffocating.

I have no idea why you have this book in your hands. Maybe you don't even know how it ended up there, let alone if you're ready for what you're about to read. I don't know if you can handle it or not at this moment in your life, so I'll get straight to the point and you can make a choice—whether you want to read on or not. (*If not, I look forward to welcoming your future self when you return.*)

The upshot is, you are responsible for you—your life and all the choices you make throughout it—not your smothering mum, over-controlling dad, estranged best friend, arsehole of an ex-partner, or society in general. Not Karen on Facebook or the stranger who put a shitty comment on your social media post, and certainly not this book.

YOU and only you.

There are a billion things in this life that you cannot change or control. Like death—we're all going to die one day, we just don't know when.

Also, whilst there are billions of things that are uncertain, there are some that are inevitable. In the space between now and then, you get to choose how you want to live and what you want to do.

It may be reassuring to know that you do have grittitude within you. Your grittitude has supreme power over all of those things (although not death; that will still happen—sorry about that). When you are aware of this, you are in the most empowered position you have ever experienced in your whole life—if you slow down and take the time and an interest in getting to know it better. You're already acquainted with your grittitude. You have it with you right now. Should you allow it, it will let you experience everything differently.

That's the bit that I do know and I am super excited to help you get to know your own grittitude better so you can develop the most amazing relationship with it.

I never believed I could write a book. So, what better way to prove my point about grittitude than by writing one, and sharing all the things that have got in my way?

I founded my business, Gritty People, over ten years ago. It was always my mission to help as many people as possible get to know themselves better, to fall in love with themselves and to be effortless with that love. Over those years (and tears), I have travelled the world delivering workshops, keynote speeches, and one-to-one coaching sessions to thousands of people. These people have been CEOs, entrepreneurs, professional athletes; children, men, and women. Grittitude is not reserved for the few. It is here for everyone should you step in and take ownership of it.

I am eternally grateful to all those people and our meaningful interactions, as I have learnt as much from them as they have from me. I want to reach more people. Everyone needs to know how empowering themselves can change the space between now and then, for the better.

I'm going to share a whole bunch of stories, all real-life experiences, followed by the bullshit we tell ourselves every day that gets in the way. We're not creating a 'new person' with 'new goals'. It's still you, just not the you whom you may have come to identify with. It's you with a different view.

Your grittitude runs everything from how you think to how you feel and behave. It's the most powerful system you will ever have to manage, yet you've never stopped to read the instruction manual. Your mind is running your entire life.

You might be wondering, 'What the hell do you know about my mind?' I know both *not much* and *a lot* all at the same time, depending on your point of view. I mean, I never used to have a great relationship with my own mind. In fact, I was so oblivious to the importance of the relationship I had with my mind that I hadn't even considered loving it. Why would I?

I was doing well in my career and navigating the day-to-day challenges of life. I thought everything was okay. Hard, but normal life is hard sometimes, especially as a dedicated working parent to two small children. It can feel like a bit of a fight for all of us, right?

That was what I thought until I was introduced to NLP (Neuro Linguistic Programming) about fourteen years ago. These three tiny letters had a massively profound impact on my life personally, professionally, and athletically. Discovering this world opened my eyes to something that I could not unsee.

This chance meeting led me to become aware of things that brought out enlightening revelations and extremely uncomfortable feelings in equal measure. I felt pain as the rawness of my reality skimmed the open wounds of my heart in ways I could have never anticipated, feelings I'd worked successfully to avoid.

It felt a bit like the dressing had been stripped away, and the open wound was vulnerable to infection. I wanted to wrap it back up as quickly as possible, sure that if I allowed myself or anyone else to go near it I would bleed to death. I saw things that made my stomach hurl, and made me want to run and hide. Yet I could not. It was like a morbid curiosity. I knew I wasn't going to like what I saw and felt compelled to take a peek anyway.

When you give yourself permission to experience both the pain and the pleasure, you will discover things that you were not looking for. These are the learnings that will stay with you forever, the learnings that get to the crux of your experience, the stuff that makes the learnings stick. There is a huge difference between knowing about something and being able to do it.

It's a bit like when you read a book on mindset, and you know 'what' to do. It's not until you start to practise the various techniques that you really learn 'how' to do it. Then, of course, real world situations provide you with the opportunity to test what you have learnt.

I don't know what you've learnt to do in the past or what you might learn to do in the future, but whatever those things are, I'm pretty sure they were different when you did it than when you read about it or were told about doing it.

Think back to being a child; you didn't learn to ride a bike from a book. With each of these chapters, read lightly and allow yourself to relate the content to your own real-life experiences.

As you read these pages, you may feel a little uncomfortable at times. The points I place before you may guide you to self-reflect, look inward, and allow your unconscious mind to explore concepts you have never before explored.

Remember, it's not only okay to feel this way—it's great! Embrace that feeling. Every time you feel it you are learning something new about yourself and others.

As children, we continuously ask questions; we enjoy the process of exploring the world around us. As adults, we tend to ask ourselves fewer important questions or even stop asking them. We stop challenging the make-up of the environment in which we live. We live our lives today with the beliefs of yesterday. Yet like the old cassette player you used to treasure so dearly, they no longer serve any meaningful, valuable purpose. You may hold on to it, but you're not going to play any new songs. Just the old ones, some of which may bring back fond memories and others less so. One thing is for sure—you won't create any new songs. You will remain stuck in the past.

Much of the challenge we face today is caused by attempting to move forward with outdated systems. In terms of our minds, I am referring to the human system.

Once you are aware of the songs that are keeping you stuck, you have a choice that will require you to make a decision:

- Keep playing it
- Stop playing it
- Change the way you play it

Take from this book the bits that work for you, leave the bits that don't, and above all else allow yourself to become curious and confused along the way.

Then we can curiously explore the answers together.

By evaluating the experience, joining in with the stories, and being open to the experience, you will develop the ability to flex your behaviour for the right situation.

The only really important questions right now are:

> *Are you happy with where you currently are?*
> *Are you willing to put in the time and effort to get where you want to be?*
> *Are you ready to start admitting your own cold, hard truths?*
> *Are you ready to develop your grittitude?*

Anything is possible. You just have to ask yourself the right questions and be willing to answer them.

Are you ready?

Love Kay xx

What if you could totally redesign your life?

INTRODUCTION

JACQUI FLAVELL

There are many books out there on changing your mindset, so what makes this one special?

It's told from very personal experiences. Not only those of Kay and me, but of all the people we have met who have changed our world along the way.

Relate these lessons to your own experiences. Our examples will help you recall the stories in your own life that illustrate the learnings for you.

Both Kay and I are passionate about helping people live their best lives. We share that. And we're also very different. We've lived very different lives and made different choices. For so long my goal was to be more like Kay. More courageous, more spontaneous, more confident. My goal was to be more like someone else.

It was a light bulb moment when I realised that I wanted to fundamentally change my nature, personality, and identity. What if, instead, I decided that it was okay to be me?

Grittitude can be introverted, considered and calm. I decided to embrace my desire to pause, plan, and prepare.

It was Christmas 2005, and I was having a crisis.

My weight was at a new all-time high and I was really fed up.

I was talking to a friend at work who had just been to an expert in NLP (Neuro Linguistic Programming) to give up smoking, and in just one session it had worked. She was now a non-smoker. I immediately started to wonder if it would work for weight loss too. I had a hundred questions. Who is he? How did you hear about him? Is it safe? And most importantly—will it work for me?

I summoned up all my courage and called him. He was very friendly and matter of fact about how simple it is and how it would work.

I was curious. And I was willing to be open-minded. At the time I lived in London, and he was in Glasgow. All I could think about was how soon I could get there. One week later I was sitting in his office feeling nervous, excited, and just a little bit sick.

What happened next changed my life in more ways than I could have ever expected.

I immediately started to lose weight. It was like he had flicked a switch inside my head that changed how I thought and felt about food. It was amazing. I discovered that there is a switch in my head for weight loss and I have the power to switch it on and off.

The only problem with this insight is that when I'm feeling stressed and emotional, I flick the switch back on as I believe that over-eating will bring me comfort. Knowing that I have done it and it was my choice is both empowering and annoying! I will, no doubt, share more about this later.

Discovering this 'switch' made me wonder whether there's also a dial for anxiety, a lever for pain, a button for happiness. This ignited a passion in me to find out what other new choices I could create with it. I learned that my brain has a dashboard, and I could learn how to reset and change my thoughts and emotions.

The answer was NLP.

This was the start of a long road of learning, discovery, and change. The more I learned, the more I wanted to share my knowledge with others.

That's why I am so excited about this book. I know that you can learn to have new thoughts and behaviours to get the life you want. All you have to do is decide you want it.

That's the offer here. Decide what you want and then commit to taking action to get it.

Sounds easy. Of course, it's not. And yet, it might just be easier than you think. And you will probably have to work no harder than you work right now doing things that you don't want to do and don't make you feel happy. And if it's important enough, you'll want to make the effort to change. That's what grittitude is all about. Having the perseverance, courage, and passion to succeed.

I'm amazed how often people find it extremely easy to answer the question, 'What don't you like about your job/relationship/life?' It seems to be something that people spend a lot of time considering and sharing. The question, 'What do you want instead?' or, 'What would make you happy?' is often met with a pause.

Stop right now and ask yourself these questions:

> *What do you want to change?*
> *What makes you happy?*
> *What would you choose if you could totally redesign your life?*

Now check your answers. Are they a list of things you want or things you don't want?

The answers are inside of you. Which is great. It also means that the problems are inside of you—as well as the opportunity to change. If you have spent your life until now blaming the outside world for your problems, I make no apology in letting you know your first cold, hard truth; that's just an excuse and it won't work anymore.

The world is a challenging and changing place and you can't control much of it. Choosing to take responsibility and accepting that all your problems and solutions are inside of you is the single most powerful lesson you can learn.

Are you ready to make a change?
Is it time for you to have the life you want?
Are you ready to choose your own life story?

Well, let's begin.

Love Jacqui xx

HOW TO USE THIS BOOK

Welcome to your book.

It is yours to do whatever you want with; we simply want to help you get the most out of it.

We will introduce you to eighteen gritty attitudes: what we call grittitudes. These are beliefs that help you see the world in a way that will give you more choices.

We will share lots of stories, knowledge and learning and we've done the hard work for you. We don't want to bog you down with loads of jargon, science, and labels. It's not our style, and it's not that kind of book.

All of our stories are based on real people that we have worked with over the years. Because we fiercely protect all of our clients' confidentiality, we have changed the names and many of the details so you can benefit from their experience while our clients remain totally protected.

We will ask questions to challenge your thinking, create new insight, and help you make the changes you want.

Some questions you may want to consider the whole way through are:

> *How am I feeling right now reading this?*
> *How does this show up in my life?*
> *What am I thinking?*
> *What is one thing I will do differently now?*
> *What pictures come to mind when I read this?*
> *What is that little voice in my head saying?*
> *How will this give me more choice?*

You could read it cover to cover and choose not to answer any of the questions. You may diligently take your time to reflect and answer all of the questions. You may want to create a grittitude journal. It's up to you. You know what works best for you.

All we ask is that you set some time aside for yourself and actually read it. The rest is up to you.

We know you have the power to change your life and achieve anything that you want. You can change your story and achieve results beyond belief.

We're just excited to be part of it.

With Love
Kay & Jacqui xx

PART 1

THE ADVENTURE STARTS HERE

Maybe right now you feel curious and excited to see where this story will take you.

Maybe you're a little afraid. What will this adventure entail? Will it get messy? Will there be times when you wish you never started?

Alice's curiosity led her to drink from the little green bottle labelled *Drink me*. She didn't know what would happen next. *Are you willing to allow your curiosity to lead you?*

We will be here to help and guide you through the epic adventure that is choosing your own life story. We start where all great adventures start: from where you are right now.

That is, after all, exactly where you are meant to be.

The journey to your destination will mean confronting who you are now, what isn't working for you, and what's stopping you from being the hero of your own story.

> **Whilst grittitude takes effort, it doesn't have to be hard.**

1

GRITTITUDE

YOU CHOOSE TO BELIEVE THAT YOU CREATE A WORLD FULL OF CHOICE

She won gold!

He's an unbeatable machine!

They are a force!

I'm not totally on board with the idea that everyone loves a success story. *Are you on board with it?*

Success stories are like Marmite. We either love to read about the guy with buckets of talent who 'got lucky' or loathe him because he 'got lucky'.

Let's be honest—the latter should really have 'when you didn't' tagged on the end. You flopped at the first thought of 'effort'. *Did you even get started?*

We've all said it at some point in our lives: 'That sounds like too much effort to me,' or, 'I don't know how they can be bothered,' or, 'I'm tired just watching them.' These are at the kinder end of the spectrum of comments, complimentary even. How about the times when you find yourself saying, 'How the hell did they get that job? They don't deserve it,' or, 'Born with a silver spoon in her mouth, that girl,' or, 'They must have paid their way in. Money talks in this place.'

Have you ever been that person?

The bitter comments are soaked in disbelief and unfairness at someone else's success.

I'm going to let you into a little secret. You can't see something in someone else that doesn't already exist within you. Perception, after all, is all anyone really has of someone else. It's simply a projection of something that exists inside of you.

Uncomfortable, right?

It's worth asking yourself this question: *What is it about them that causes your own perceptions to be projected so strongly?* Then notice how what you see in them actually brings up something in you.

The triumph of an overnight sensation tends to trigger a cocktail of emotions in people. Depending on the illusions of the mind, you don't see anything how it really is; you see it from a perspective of how you really are. We all read stories of people in the public eye who have 'appeared on the scene'. Some 'big hitter' arrives at the office making a massive impact in just a few months. An athlete makes the team or stands on the podium whilst you look around wondering where the hell they came from.

Do you decide there must be some dodgy reason for their success? They are a cheater; they have a rich family… failing or refusing to see the real reason they have triumphed—they were always there in the background, working hard, being consistent, struggling, putting the effort into their belief that one day they will fulfil their promise to their self. They did all this in the deep knowing that they would one day achieve their goals and dreams.

The underdog was always there, working silently, making their way forward, one step, lap, meeting, or late night at a time. You didn't see them because you were so focused on the people at the front before them, either sharing in or seething at their success. There's immense power in the opportunity to struggle. The only way a butterfly has of strengthening its wings enough to use them to fly is to struggle through the process of releasing itself. If we were to 'help' the butterfly out, we would be cheating it of the one opportunity it has to strengthen itself and complete its metamorphosis. A butterfly that doesn't get this opportunity will not be strong enough to fly and live its life purpose.

There is often a deep desire to jump in and 'save' those we love, yet there is greater power in allowing them to be supported as they live and learn how to strengthen their own wings.

Life presents struggle. This is a given. As you grow, you transform, and as you move forward through the different stages of your life's story, you will without doubt experience periods of struggle punctuated by breakthroughs to greater self-awareness, and the shedding of beliefs that no longer serve you.

Having grittitude is not easy, and it's absolutely not lucky. Grittitude requires effort, determination and knowing what your dreams and goals are. It requires you to know why you are pursuing them and to stick with them, despite the multitude of setbacks and struggles that will inevitably knock you down along the way.

The athlete waking with the larks to get training in before work, missing evening parties with friends or lazy evenings in front of the fire: that's who you are watching compete; that's why it means so much.

The person who has lost their job and feels like a failure, worrying about the future: that's who you just offered a job to.

The teenager selling sweets from their school bag in the hope of making a few pence or pounds instead of playing games during break-time: that's who just became the first person you know who started their own business.

Real success is gained through a beautifully messy recipe of many ingredients coming together, often after many failed attempts, tears, and fears along the way.

Having a gritty attitude and approach to life is *grittitude*.

Grittitude takes perseverance. There are some behaviours that you will do easily and effortlessly and others that you will avoid. Imagine it like different pieces of equipment in the gym. When you walk in you may naturally gravitate toward a particular one. Like the running machine or free weights section... and others you do everything in your power to avoid. For you, maybe it's the mountain climber; man, that thing makes your thighs burn! Of course, the more you do something the better you get at it.

Are you getting better at negative or positive behaviours?

Jacqui's Story – The Move

When I was fifteen, we moved house. My dad had a great opportunity to do what he loved, and that meant relocating. It's hard to be happy for your parents when you're a kid. I was so wrapped up in everything that was important to me at the time. I wasn't happy for my dad; I was devastated for me.

My friends had a leaving party for me, which further reinforced how happy I was with my life, my friends, my school. It had never occurred to me that I wouldn't live in Reigate for my whole life.

We moved to Oxford. It should have been great. It was a big new city, and my parents were excited. It was a new chapter for them. There would be more money and a better life; they bought their first house; they were happy.

My brother seemed to settle in about five minutes. I did not.

I was not a rebellious child. I wasn't brave or intrepid. There was a limit to what I had in my arsenal to show my unhappiness. But I was convinced that if they could see how unhappy I was, they would pack us all up and move back 'home'.

My first line of attack was the hunger strike. That's probably a bit dramatic, but I did stop eating. I doubt that I was ever in real peril, and it took a while for anyone to notice. We went out for Sunday lunch, and I announced, 'I am not eating that.'

My dad's response was, 'Oh yes, you bloody well are, and we're sitting here until you do.' So I did. I told you I wasn't cut out to be a rebel. It was then, looking back, that I turned to food to fill the hole.

School was the other domain I could control. It was a girls' school, which only added to the feeling that nothing was the same. I decided to simply not fit in. Not make friends. Not try.

I was already into the two-year run-up to my exams and my grades were nose-diving. It didn't matter. I didn't care.

The following summer I went 'home'. I spent the long holiday staying with friends back in Reigate. They had a welcome back party for me this time. I was happy.

Then it all went wrong. My old school was due to start back two days before mine in Oxford. I had a brilliant idea. I would go back to my old school for the first day in September. I would have my old life back for one day: my old school, my old friends, my old teachers; I could travel back in time.

To this day, I am not sure what I expected when I walked back in... bunting, flags, balloons, cheers of *we've all missed you sooo much!*? That is not what I got. What happened was they all started to talk about what they had done in the summer. They had made new social groups; some of my friends were now dating each other; they had started smoking: everything had changed. I didn't fit in.

I was devastated. I had the realisation that, if I got my wish, if we moved back, it would be as hard for me to fit back in here as it was in Oxford. Unable to stop the tears, I left immediately, went back to my friend's house, packed my bag and got the coach home.

On the coach, I made a choice. A decision. I decided that I had to change. I lived in Oxford now. That was home. I had to make a life there. I had to change my story.

I had one year to drag my grades back from crap to just about average.

I made it work. And of course, when I look back, I can see the opportunity that it was. It changed me for the better. It taught me that I had control after all. I could choose to make it a success or a failure.

Since then, I have moved many more times. I have lived in six counties and worked all over the world. Home is where I am right now, not one fixed place on a map.

That girl who was certain she would live her whole life in Reigate would be proud of where I ended up, even though it is less than fifty miles from where I began.

> **Choice is the only thing
> that is not a choice.
> Choice is a given.
> Choice is a birth right.**

Whilst GRITTITUDE takes effort, it doesn't have to be hard

As a society, we often measure success on talent. We get excited about natural talent; we have shows like *Britain's Got Talent*; most organisations have 'talent pools/groups'. The word itself is thrown around mindlessly. You would be forgiven for thinking that talent is the only predictor of success.

But what's talent without grittitude? You can be the most 'naturally talented' person in the world and if you don't show up day after day, moment after moment, talent means very little. It's not about how you manage success. Grittitude is about how you manage failure. It is about coming up against obstacles over and over again and still moving forward with unwavering determination. It's sticking with your future, not just for days, or weeks but for years, a collection of 'one moments'.

Talent has had its airtime. It's time to let grittitude out into the light

Have you ever had a time when you faced adversity? A time when the odds were stacked against you and on paper you just 'shouldn't' have succeeded? And somehow, some way, you found a way through?

That's Grittitude.

Grittitude is a choice. The common theme throughout this book is that you have a choice in how you behave. We can share with you the attitudes, skills and beliefs that will help you to achieve your goals. *You* still have to choose to take them. There's an old saying: 'You can lead a horse to water, but you can't make it drink.' Just to be clear, you're the horse.

Throughout this adventure, we will let you know some useful beliefs. These are the eighteen grittitudes that will change the way you see the world and may change the way you live in it.

Mind Full or Mindful?

It's mid-afternoon on a beautiful sunny day, and I'm driving on a country road with a speed limit of 40 mph. I am therefore driving at 40 mph. The car behind me is right up my arse, and the driver has spent the last few minutes swerving slightly into the middle of the road attempting to overtake.

Each time, a car appears on the opposite side of the road and he reluctantly backs away, until in a heartbeat he makes the decision to go.

Shit! There's a car coming the other way, and it's too late for him to back off this time. He's committed.

I brake to create space. The car heading right toward the overtaking car slams on the brakes heavily. He makes it back onto the right side of the road in front of me with a split second to spare.

I didn't realise I'd been holding my breath, but I was, and as I breathe out, taking a moment to check I really am still alive, I arrive at the traffic lights. They are on red.

The overtaking driver risked my life, their life, the lives of the driver and passenger of the other car—to progress by the grand distance of a car's length.

We could choose to believe that the driver had a really important place to be. Perhaps their house was on fire or a loved one was in the hospital. That may be true or untrue in this particular situation. I also observe that sort of behaviour every day, whether I'm driving to work, walking the dogs, or having a conversation. The world is in such a rush.

Part of my frustration with this is that I see an old version of myself in that behaviour. I used to cram as much as possible into every day, never stopping to enjoy experiences, always thinking ahead to the next challenge or task. Often when we talk about grittitude there's an association with being tough, which is indeed true, yet there's no way to be tough without being gentle too, and it doesn't mean you never slow down or stop. It isn't possible to persevere, stay resilient and remain high in energy if you spend all your energy on things that don't matter and will eventually slow you down anyway.

Kay's Story – Ward 40

After an operation requiring bed rest, I refused to stay in hospital overnight as I needed to get to my son's school performance that evening and more importantly (to me at that time) to work the following day. I was so concerned that I might lose a contract with a new client if I took the day off, I wouldn't entertain the thought of having time to rest and heal. I carried on and ignored every signal to stop and rest that my body was screaming at me.

Four days later, from the side of the football pitch during Saturday league, I was rushed into hospital. Things had gone wrong, and I was told it was critical. I stayed in for urgent care. This was followed by four weeks of bed rest. Four weeks of absolutely nothing. My mind could not compute this idea. How was it even possible that people could just sit down and do nothing? The only time I did that was to sleep. The doctor agreed to let me leave the ward if my husband promised to make sure I did nothing. That was a mammoth task and he knew it.

Everything I had been trying to avoid happened, only ten times worse. I lost my health, those who love me had all the worry, and I lost the contract.

During my recovery, I had time to reflect.

That overtaking car was dangerous, and he will get grief for his actions, and I'm sure you would agree. Yet, what we do to ourselves every day is dangerous too. The only difference is that we dress it up in self-importance and a bullshit story about how we 'haven't got time'.

We all have the same twenty-four hours in every day. When you panic about how much time you have left, you risk missing out on so much in an attempt to get somewhere a few minutes earlier, get that next promotion a few years sooner, reach the peak of your athletic career a few months younger. At what cost?

When you decide not to rush, panic and sacrifice to the point of illness, it does not mean you will never achieve your goals and dreams. It may mean you do get to enjoy the adventure and the destination when you arrive.

It's your twenty-four hours. You choose how you spend it.

Signals

Need a wee?

Feeling hungry?

Thirsty?

How do you know?

You get a signal from your amazing body to your mind, a feeling that's a signal that you need to go to the toilet, eat something, or drink something, and you mostly respond.

Pain, mental or physical, is a signal.

You have time: are you being mindful about how and where you spend it?

You have signals: are you responding to them?

Rehearse

Practice makes perfect... Does it really?

How do you know?

What does perfect really mean?

Does perfect exist?

How do you know your idea of perfect and mine are the same?

How do I know mine and yours are the same?

What are you comparing it to?

What does good look like?

So many questions!

There is sound evidence that 'ten thousand hours of intense practice create mastery' but even Malcolm Gladwell never used the word 'perfect'.[1]

Perfect is a unicorns and rainbows idea of the world; it's lovely and wildly unrealistic. The very idea of being perfect is someone else's idea of an ideal, a picture they have in their mind. It may be their idea of perfection and not match yours. Does that make it wrong? Of course not. It makes it different. Equally, multiple people could have a similar idea of the outcome they want and a completely different way of getting theirs. Does that make one way wrong? Of course not. It makes it different.

Rehearsal, however, is something we can all do. Rehearsing with intent will focus our attention on being specific about what we want to get better at.

Like sex, the more you do it the better you get at it.

Rehearsal 'with intent' is what really makes the difference, whether that's mentally or physically. When we have a clear intention for our rehearsal, it creates a strong context and framework for what we are doing so we fully engage in the activity, whether that's in work, sport, mindfulness, sex, or simply learning something new.

Fire in your heart

If you don't have passion for what you are doing, you're not going to keep persevering, and if you don't have the energy to persevere, you're not going to be able to keep the fire of passion burning bright within you. In my daily work, I am contacted by people who feel completely bemused. They say,

'It's like a switch has gone off,' or, 'The fire has gone out.' The light to that fire, the flick to that switch, is passion.

Uncovering your true passion in life is not reserved for a select few. A person full of passion can be seen from miles around. You know when you've met one and you know when you are one. Because the feeling of passion is so powerful, you also know when it's gone, and it can be upsetting, confusing and frustrating not knowing where to find it. It is like misplacing your keys to a door behind which lies all that you need to get moving.

What do you love to do? I mean *really* love to do. Not kind of like, or enjoy because you think you should, not what you have been brought up being told you should be grateful for, or who you should be, or how you should behave.

What brings you alive from the inside?

What makes your face bright and your eyes sparkle when you think or talk about it?

What makes you want to get up early because you know you're doing that thing that day?

What do you do even if it's not easy because there's a fire burning deep inside telling you it just feels right?

Answer these questions from your heart and you'll discover the true meaning of passion in a much more powerful, meaningful, and relatable way than the written word could ever achieve.

My all-time favourite quote is by Teddy Roosevelt from an address he made over one hundred years ago. His words are as true now as the day they were spoken. [2]

> "It is not the critic who counts; not the man who points out how the strong man stumbles or where the doer of deeds could have done better.
>
> **The credit belongs to the man who is actually in the arena, whose face is marred by dust and sweat and blood; who strived valiantly; who errs, who comes again and again, because there is no effort without error and shortcoming;** but who does actually strive to do the deeds; who knows great enthusiasms, the great devotions; who spends himself in a worthy cause; who at the best knows in the end the triumph of high achievement, and who at the worst, if he fails, at least fails while daring greatly."

TEDDY ROOSEVELT

2

THE ATLAS

YOU CHOOSE TO BELIEVE EVERYONE HAS THEIR OWN MAP OF THE WORLD

What's your dream holiday destination?

Take a moment and allow your mind to travel there right now...

It might be somewhere you have already been or somewhere you have dreamed of going.

What can you see?

What can you hear?

How do you feel?

Where did you go? Maybe you went somewhere cold and snowy and yet, I wouldn't be surprised if you just popped off to St Lucia, Barbados, Costa Rica or the Bahamas, somewhere you can pretty much guarantee blue skies, sandy beaches, turquoise seas, and palm trees waving in the breeze.

If you live in the UK with our unpredictable weather and often non-existent summers, the draw of tropical islands can feel like paradise.

The reality, however, for many of the people who live in these 'luxury' travel destinations is extreme poverty and very poor living conditions. Of course, the only people from around the world they get to see are those who can afford to travel to these far-flung destinations.

I've been fortunate enough to travel all around the world and it still shocks me that I can walk just a mile from those five-star hotels and perfect beaches to find poverty and destruction.

Looking through the eyes of the people living in these conditions, I see tourists come for short stays, enjoying five-star treatment and I get the perception that everyone who lives abroad has plenty of money and an easy life.

When I look through my own eyes, I see sadness and poverty.

When I step into the role of the tour guides, hoteliers, and business owners I see gratitude for the money being brought to the island by a thriving tourist trade.

As I walk through these three positions and look through each lens, my view of the world changes too. It expands, and it gives me more choice.

We all think we live in the same world. It is true of course that we do all live in the same physical world.

We do not share the same *view* of the world and nor do we share the experiences we have within it. Each and every one of us is experiencing the world in our own unique way.

Starting to recognise that what goes on in your experience of the world is greatly dependent on what is going on inside your own head and less dependent on what is going on out there will massively shift how you think about every single thing that you say and do. You have much more choice, control, and power over your thoughts, actions, and outcomes than you may realise. Of course, things happen in the world that are outside of your control, and yet by focusing on all of the things that are 100% within your control – your thoughts and actions – you have much greater control over your experiences and outcomes.

You could continue to think that the people who achieve great things are lucky, or have had things handed to them, and maybe some of that is true, yet that isn't helpful to you. *What if, instead, you choose to believe that you have the opportunity to achieve whatever you put your mind to?*

We will share with you the gritty attitudes: what we call grittitudes. These are beliefs that help you see the world in a way that will give you more choices. If you find yourself thinking, saying, or feeling that you can't choose your own life story, you can't achieve your dreams, you can't be successful, or even seemingly small things like the time you 'have to' get up in the morning to travel to work, or 'have to' do the housework, or the school run, or in fact anything that you don't want to do, then hold on to your hat, because understanding these beliefs better and choosing to live by them is going to change your life!

Experience and research tell us these are the beliefs that 'successful' people operate from, whether they are aware of it or not. Remember that we are not saying they are necessarily true. They may not be true. But then all beliefs are neither true nor untrue, more a narrative that we run in our minds and then we act as though they are true.

Beliefs are the world's best storytellers…

Let's start with a random example. If I believe that steak should be cooked medium-rare… does that make me right? or wrong? I guess that's going to depend on your beliefs. If you love a medium-rare steak, you will be nodding and smiling in complete agreement right now. If you're a well-done kind of person, your forehead may be furrowed as you read these words, shaking your head, or perhaps you are vegetarian and feel disgusted at the suggestion of eating steak at any stage of the cooking process?

And what if you don't have a narrative? What if you have never tasted steak before? In fact, what if you have never tasted meat before? You have no point of reference in this particular context. You have no narrative at all. Nothing to compare it to.

Your best friend says, 'What! You've never had steak? It's amazing; it tastes delicious, and you must have it medium rare. It tastes so much nicer cooked that way.' Already the narrative is evolving. They are excited. You trust them. You take a mouthful and as you are well primed with a positive experience narrative, your taste buds respond and look for this beautiful taste you have been expecting. 'Wow,' you find yourself saying. 'This is amazing, so juicy, and tasty; it's delicious.'

On the other hand, you have the other friend who has just taken a bite of their steak, and you've watched their face screw up as they convulse at the taste of what they have just put in their mouth. They turn to you and say, 'Oh my god, that tastes awful... taste it...'

No thanks!

As we walk you through these narratives, instead of worrying about whether or not they are true, focus on whether or not this new narrative will allow you to get the results you want.

Everyone sees the world differently, but you already know this, right? Of course you do. You know because you've had disagreements, arguments, and deep frustrations when someone has seen the same situation in a completely different way to you.

You've also had moments of realisation, light bulb moments when someone has said something that's made you say, 'Oh, I've never thought of it like that.'

Once we are brought into this world, we all have a different way of experiencing the world, different parents, with different beliefs, values, cultures, environments, social environments, financial access, and rewards. From childhood, we are incredibly heavily influenced by all of those things and so, of course, we are all unique and different. We all see and experience this world differently.

Respect that.

When anyone disagrees with you, has an opposite point of view, or is rude or intolerant, remind yourself there is a good chance they are not actually being a prick on purpose. They are simply being active with their view of the world, and it doesn't match yours.

No two people experience any event in the same way, so we are all creating our own maps of the world all the time. It's quite cool, really. We are all navigating the same planet but we are each working from our own atlas.

How often have you talked to someone, a friend or family member, about an event that happened years ago, and you both have a totally different memory about it? Maybe something that was really significant for you was easily forgotten by them, or you totally disagree about what took place at all.

From steak to holiday destinations, we all live in our own unique little bubble.

No matter how hard to understand another person's behaviour is, it is simply their experience of the world. Take an extreme example of someone who is being violent: could you say for sure, that if you had only experienced what they had experienced, learnt what they had learned, seen, heard, and felt what they had, you would not behave in exactly the same way? The truth is, you couldn't know, because no one could.

Try to see things from the other person's point of view. Have patience with them. Accept that your point of view is simply that – your point of view, and they will have their own. They are not doing it to annoy you. Unless they are, and then they must have a reason for wanting to annoy you. Or maybe that's just the meaning you're placing on their actions.

Sometimes you'll meet people who appear to be 'on the same page' as you. They share your values and beliefs on a particular topic, and you share theirs. The connection feels obvious and strong. You share the same page on the Atlas.

Nish's Story

Nish worked for the fleet maintenance team in a large corporate business. It was our first session.

I asked what they would like to focus on. They said that the part of the job that was most stressful was calling clients to give them updates on when their vehicles would be ready for collection.

They said, 'Most of the clients are ok, but one of the companies is a nightmare. Every time they call in to get an update, they are rude, aggressive and angry, every single one of them.'

I said that I was surprised that every employee in one specific company would be like that. I said that I doubted they had a hiring policy of only recruiting people who were angry, aggressive assholes. From Nish's face, I got the impression they hadn't thought about this before. I said, 'I wonder if there is any common thread that explains why all these particular clients react that way.'

Nish paused for a moment then said, 'Actually, I think I did hear that when these drivers' vehicles are off the road, they don't get paid for those days. I suppose that could have something to do with it!'

We talked for a few minutes about how it would impact Nish if every time their vehicle needed servicing or repair, they didn't get paid. They said that it would probably make them worried, frustrated and angry. Bingo.

I asked what impact this realisation could have on how Nish managed the calls. They said they could see it from their point of view now and could empathise with how they are feeling and even be prepared to put up with a bit of their anger. We discussed phrases they could use such as, 'I know this is difficult for you... I promise it will be done as soon as possible so you can get back on the road... I know this isn't what you want to hear, and I am sorry it is going to take longer than you thought.'

I asked what they had learned from seeing the situation from a different perspective. They agreed that it had made them think and they would try to picture the person on the end of the phone next time they had to deliver a difficult message.

―――

If you know your map is different from my map, how can we still go on this adventure together?

How will your life change if you choose to see things from other people's points of view?

What if you remembered that your point of view is simply that, your point of view?

Don't Say Don't.

3

DON'T READ THIS CHAPTER
YOU CHOOSE TO BELIEVE IN THE POWER OF LANGUAGE

No, seriously, don't read it.

It's only important if you want to really understand how much power and choice you can have over your thoughts, emotions, and behaviours. You probably don't need to know about that, do you?

You don't need to know that NLP was developed in the 1970s by John Grinder and Richard Bandler, or that their work was based on earlier work and research into mindset, psychology, and hypnotherapy. Nor do you need to know that it is a collection of ideas, patterns, and techniques that will help you make changes in your work, sport, and life.

We mentioned NLP earlier and knew you wouldn't be curious about it. If Richard or John were here now, they would be banging on about how *Neuro* relates to the brain, *Linguistics* connects to the language we use every day, and *Programming* puts it all together as a way of doing things. But they are not here or responsible for these words, so we're not going to mention it.

As we said, you don't need to know any of that, so instead, we are going to explore self-talk and non-verbal communication.

Wait a moment... how rude of us. We are all this way into this adventure, and we haven't even asked how you are doing. *How are you doing?*

Mustn't grumble.

I'm not too bad.

Could be worse.

Wow. What hope is there for a positive mindset if that's not only what you think, it's what you say to people who simply ask, 'How are you doing?'

The things you say are being heard by you too. Are they helpful or hurtful?

If you tell yourself, 'I'm no good,' often enough, you will start to believe it to be true. Which is pretty silly, really. Perhaps you're not the best person to listen to advice from. If you want to know about nutrition you would ask a nutritionist, right? If you want to learn how to be a better CEO you might ask a great CEO for advice. So, what makes you think you're an expert on whether you're 'good enough' at life? You're not the expert so why are you listening to crappy advice from yourself? If you're going to make up a story about whether you're good enough or not, you might as well make it a good one.

"**Whether you think you can, or think you can't – you're right**"

HENRY FORD

Everything we do starts with a thought, and in the grand scheme of things those tiny packets of information are pretty important.

In the military, there is a commander, and that commander has a pretty big responsibility. They go through years of training and gain experience in order to become the person responsible for supervision and decision-making. They will give instructions in a hostile situation which could be the difference between life and death for the men and women in the platoon under their command.

Your conscious mind is the commander. That means *you* are the commander. I know you didn't ask for this job and perhaps you would prefer not to have it but it's yours. The way your conscious mind talks and makes decisions has a direct impact on how you behave. Your unconscious mind is the platoon under its command. It is just doing as it is told.

Your unconscious mind doesn't have the ability, training or experience to make decisions. It is, however, responsible for all your behaviours and works on autopilot twenty-four hours a day unless the commander (your conscious mind) gives it a new command.

When the commander uses negative language, it's giving a negative goal command, and the unconscious mind has no way of knowing if it's the right thing to do or not, it simply follows the command.

If it hears, 'Be grumpy,' it automatically responds with, 'Right team: the commander says it's time to be grumpy.' The unconscious mind will then activate that battle plan. Operation Grumpy activated.

If it hears, 'I can do this,' it automatically responds with, 'Right team: the commander says it's time to do this.' The unconscious mind will then activate *that* battle plan. Operation We Can Do This.

We can change our behaviours. We simply have to consciously train the mind to use language in a different way. Then you will change your results.

> **"Our thoughts become things"**

This is why positive affirmations are so powerful.

You know the ones – the wooden, hand-painted boards hung up with a piece of string that make such popular (if cheesy) gifts.

Live. Laugh. Love.

Life isn't about waiting for the storm to pass... It's learning to dance in the rain.

If life gives you lemons, make lemonade.

You can scoff at these affirmations, but where's the harm? What's the alternative?

Die, cry into your coffee, hate.

Speak to yourself differently. Say, 'I'm brilliant, and I can achieve anything,' and notice what changes in your life.

It sounds too good to be true, but it really works. Start to notice the specific positive and negative words you use in everyday language.

When the words you say to yourself have so much impact on you, why wouldn't you want to be as positive as possible?

We do it to other people too.

Imagine a friend sends you a message saying, 'Are you free later? Can I call you this afternoon?'

Let's say you reply, 'No problem.'

What do you think they are thinking now?

Your response was positive. You were saying *yes*. But funnily enough, you *didn't* say yes.

You said *no problem*. Think about that for a second; your two-word response was a combination of *no* and *problem*. Two **negative** words. What a strange way to say yes.

And the other person's brain may be struggling with processing *no* and *problem* as a positive response. They might even be thinking that it is a problem and you're just being polite.

No problem is a negative command to their commander. You are now relying on their commander's ability to translate those two words into something positive before the message gets relayed to their platoon. Which is crazy, right? If you sent an email or letter you wouldn't think, 'I'll write the opposite of what I mean and hope they translate it into what I really mean.'

Watch out for the negative words that find their way into your conversations. Not only will the other person question what you really mean but you are doubling down on the negative language your own platoon is hearing.

Shall we play around with some more examples?

No need to worry = Do I need to worry?

No trouble = This is trouble

That's great = That's great

It's easy = It's easy

I'd love to = I'd love to

Everything is going to plan = Everything is going to plan

Have a look back through some of your recent message exchanges. Try to find some examples of this in action.

What you see is what you get.

 "Float like a butterfly, sting like a bee"

Muhammed Ali, in our opinion the world's greatest boxer, consistently rehearsed an incredibly powerful technique. Today we would call it visualisation. The all-time great liked to call it 'Future History'. Visualisation is a term often used without a real understanding of what it means or how it works. It stretches way beyond simply 'imagining' you can do something or have done something. The visualisation is the trigger.

You see something you want to happen in your mind. This triggers a thought, which triggers a feeling, which triggers a physiological state change, which triggers a behaviour... which triggers an outcome.

We tend to think that the first thing that has changed is the behaviour, and this simply isn't true. Looking from the outside in, the behaviour change is what the on-lookers see. Great leadership in life and sport always starts with great leadership of self. If you want to be the best, you must first see, hear and feel like the best.

> **"Great leadership starts with great leadership of self"**

In the run-up to a fight, Muhammed would see a picture of himself at the end of the fight, arms lifted high in the air, the referee announcing him as the champion. More than this, he would see it in such bright and real light, with complete commitment and belief as though he was really there and it was really happening in that moment. Muhammed would hear the roar of the crowd and experience the feeling throughout his body as they chanted his name over and over again.

Because he had already won the fight in his mind many times, his unconscious mind had a strong and clear goal command. In his mind, he had already won.

Visualisation creates new pathways in our minds so the challenge we are about to face is not new. Because Muhammed had done this same visualisation so many times, his mind no longer knew if he had done it before or not. What could have felt challenging had become a clear and definite path to success.

Don't think of a pink elephant eating a blue banana on a beach

Firstly, you might be wondering how you just managed to think of a pink elephant eating a blue banana on a beach. Perhaps you've watched a lot of children's cartoons lately but if not, relax; I'll explain.

As long as you have seen the colours pink and blue, an elephant, a banana, a beach and someone eating, your brain will do the rest for you. It will visually construct the image. It's also why we humans are so brilliant at visualisation. If you want to stand on the top step of the podium, holding a great big trophy with everyone around you clapping and smiling, as long as you know what a podium looks like, what a trophy looks like, what clapping sounds like and what people are like when they smile, your mind will do the rest for you. Cool, right?

But remember, we have moved on from visualising. I asked you *not* to think of a pink elephant eating a blue banana on a beach.

If I say, 'Don't think of an elephant,' I **know** that you **had** to think of an elephant, even for half a second, so you knew what it was that you weren't supposed to think about!

Here's the thing...

Your brain cannot process the negative. It hears *think of an elephant* and the *don't* is an afterthought. It has to think about it to then not think about it – exhausting.

It's okay. There is another way...

Consider how many times you say *don't*.

Don't give up.
Don't be late.
Don't get nervous.
Don't forget to drink water.

What your brain hears is:

Give up.
Be late.
Get nervous.
Forget to drink water.

If you only take one lesson from this chapter let it be this: say what you do want to happen, not what you don't.

Some positive frames to use could be:

Remember to get your tickets.
Be on time.
Stay calm.
Drink water.

Notice yourself as you use phrases which include the word *don't*. This has the potential to make you crazy for a while so make it fun. Start by simply noticing when you say these phrases and just make a mental note. Then start catching yourself saying them whilst you're saying them, stop, and restate the sentence. Over a short period of time, you will change your language and become unconsciously competent as you will have reprogrammed your unconscious mind with new language to use.

You'll start to be a language ninja.

Unintentional negativity is everywhere. And once it's on your radar you will see it everywhere.

There is the recruitment poster that says, 'Why not join us?' when I am pretty sure they don't want a list of reasons why you shouldn't join. What they actually wanted to say was, 'Join us.'

There is also the missing cat poster that says, 'Lost cat, missing since Sunday.' Call me crazy... I would rather put positivity out there into the world and choose, 'Find my cat,' instead.

A whole world of possibilities

'Have you finished that book?'
'No.'

'Shall we run a 10K?'
'I can't.'

'Have you been to Australia?'
'No.'

'Can you speak another language?'
'I can't.'

'Have you ever won a competition?'
'No.'

In between the simplicity of saying what we can do and can't do, between what we want and don't want, we have the subtle art of possibility. One of the most important and undervalued words for opening up to a whole new way of thinking about challenges and new opportunities is the short and simple word *yet*.

Adding *yet* to a phrase can totally change it from a mindset of negativity to a mindset of possibility. If you do find yourself saying a negative phrase such as, 'I don't know how to do it,' or, 'I'm not good at that,' always encourage yourself to add the word *yet*.

'I don't know how to do it *yet*.'
'I'm no good at that *yet*.'
'I can't do it *yet*.'
'Not *yet*.'

This simple trick tells your unconscious mind that it's possible – you just haven't figured it out *yet*. It tells your platoon that you need to practise more and then you'll be able to do it. There are thousands of things that you couldn't do until you learned how to do them through practice, like walking, talking, tying your shoelaces, and riding a bike. Just think about the last time you achieved something you never thought you would. There was always a moment of *yet*.

We are driven forward or backward by other people's negativity. If someone tells you that you can't do something, you might react by saying, 'Okay. I won't try. You don't believe I can so you must be right.' Alternatively, you might say, 'Fuck you! Just watch me!'

I'm a *just watch me* kind of girl myself.

Please don't tell me that *you* are the person telling you that you can't do it. *Are you?*

If you're going to be your own worst enemy, don't bother reading about how you can change that. You probably really enjoy tearing yourself down and stopping yourself from being the best you can be. It's probably much more comfortable, right? If the feeling of comfort is getting a bit tedious and you want to live better, you would be wise to take some advice from Yoda in *The Empire Strikes Back*.

"Do or do not; there is no try"

You'll hear lots of people saying that you shouldn't say *try* as it presupposes failure or an acceptance that it may not be possible. *Try* can mean so many things and can be replaced easily with much more empowering alternatives. 'I will try my best,' can become, 'I will do my best.'

Your unconscious mind is listening all the time. It listens to all the negative things you say out loud about yourself, it listens to the negative thoughts you have in your head, and it listens when you direct your words at other people.

In the *Grittitude* chapter, you read about those people who choose to be negative about other people's successes. Their negativity plays a big part in limiting their own success too. If your friend tells you that they are going to attempt something amazing and you say or think, 'That sounds ridiculous. You won't make it. You'll fail,' your mind decides that you won't attempt anything like that because you don't want to be ridiculous or fail.

Even if you don't want to be positive for that person, do it for yourself. Encourage and support other people's goals and achievements, and you will hear yourself encouraging and supporting yourself.

NLP reminds us to choose both our words and our thoughts wisely. We have to start with our language to effect positive change in our brains and our thinking. By changing your words, you change your results. Start to notice the power of the language you use and hear others use.

However... we know you haven't bothered to read this chapter, so you won't have seen any of this.

Jacqui's Story - Asking For Favours

It seems to be a very British thing to make it easy for people to say no. Maybe we don't want people to feel uncomfortable. Maybe we just want to keep our expectations low. Maybe it's just habit.

Have you ever asked a favour of someone by saying, 'I don't suppose you could get this done for me today?' or, 'You couldn't help me out, could you?' and maybe, 'You haven't, by any chance, got an upgrade available, have you?'

How easy does it become for the person in each scenario to answer, 'No, you're absolutely right, I can't/couldn't/haven't.'

You won't be upset – you never really thought there was a chance anyway.

I love the movie *Shirley Valentine*. It's all about a middle-aged woman who decides she's had enough and walks out on her husband and her life to go on holiday in Greece. She has imagined herself sitting at a table by the sea, drinking a glass of wine. When she gets there, she finds a bar and asks if she could move the table right down to the water's edge. She explains about her dream. The bar owner, in a gorgeous Greek accent says, 'If I carry the table to the water, I make your dream come true?'

And that's the thing. Why wouldn't he? Who would pass up the opportunity to make someone's dream come true with such a simple act?

Do it. Next time you want someone to do you a favour, even a small one, say, 'I'd love it if you could…'

I'd love it if you could get me a table with a view.
It would mean so much to me if you could get me an upgrade.
It'd really help me out if you could get this done for me today.

And of course, you have to mean it. You can't just trot it out like the words themselves are magic.

I once put an ad online for a sofa bed I wanted to get rid of, and I offered it for free. Within minutes I had ten replies. Most just said when they could pick it up, but one said that she had just moved into a new flat and couldn't afford a sofa or a bed and if she could have this it would make her day. We had a winner!

You will find that the opportunity to do something that will make someone's day is very tempting to many people. It certainly is to me.

The amazing team I worked with turned this positive language thing into a sport. When we went out for dinner, we would try to get a round of drinks on the house by simply asking for it. We'd ask for the manager and say, 'The food was amazing. What would make the evening perfect would be to finish it with a round of shots. We'd love it if you could do that for us.'

We got it surprisingly often. And they got our repeat business, again and again.

We know you found this chapter brilliant because it's full of brilliant information that you can use straight away. How do we know you read it, even though we started out by saying, 'Don't read this chapter'?

Because you dropped the *don't*. What your mind saw was an instruction to read this chapter. Confused yet? Great! Stay curious...

Here's a recap:

- Don't say *don't*.
- Say what you do want.
- Open up a world of possibility by saying *yet*.
- Visualise what you want the future to look like.
- You are the commander.

You are part of the problem.

4

COLD, HARD TRUTHS

YOU CHOOSE TO BELIEVE YOU HAVE THE ABILITY TO INFLUENCE YOUR WORLD

If you were hoping that this book contained easy answers, a simple list of dos and don'ts that would change your life, then hopefully realisation is starting to dawn.

The answer isn't 'out there' because the problem isn't 'out there'.

The problem is you

And that might sound harsh, but trust me, it's great news. If the problem was out there then so would be the solution. It would be outside of your hands, outside of your control. By accepting that the problem is inside of you, that you are part of the problem, it puts the opportunity to fix the problem in your hands too.

So, if you're sitting comfortably, and even if you're not, are you ready for some cold, hard truths?

You are a liar

Liar, Liar.

If you haven't seen it, it's a film starring Jim Carrey all about not being able to lie for twenty-four hours. After letting his son down for the last time, the little boy makes a wish that his dad can't lie, and the wish comes true. The premise of the story reminds me of all the lies we tell ourselves and others every day. Sure, we relabel them as really good reasons; they are lies.

- I can't be as good as him: he's got more experience.
- She's better at that than me because she's got better equipment.
- They always get there first because they don't have kids to sort out.

But what if those reasons are actually lies dressed up as excuses, and wrapped in a great big bow called reasons, to make yourself more comfortable with the fact that you are telling lies to yourself?

Not only do we have our own internal voice letting us get away with the lies, we're also likely to have plenty of people around us endorsing and reinforcing that bullshit too!

What if you stopped lying to yourself?
What if you stopped lying to others?
What would you be left with?

The truth!

It would appear to be true that whenever you set yourself a task or goal, you either get the result you want or you have a lie waiting in the wings ready to whip out to excuse yourself for not achieving it. It's one of the only areas where I would suggest there is no grey area to explore. It is totally black and white.

Some people say they do not lie, they do not make excuses, they just have 'really good reasons'!

A reason, even a very good one, stops you from getting the result. So let me reframe my language. *Is what you're doing stopping you from achieving what you want?* Call it a lie, a reason, or an excuse, we don't have to be too precious about the label. If it's getting in the way of you moving forward, then it needs to go.

Think about *The Apprentice*, a reality show where twelve hopefuls compete to receive investment from Sir Alan Sugar to start their own business. Sir Alan creates two teams and sets them a task. There is a winning and a losing team.

Sometimes the 'losing' team loses by just a few pounds. They always have good reasons. As far as Sir Alan is concerned, they are simply excuses. He doesn't care what the excuse is; it simply didn't get the desired outcome.

Consider all the 'lies' you use. *You may or may not have lots of them, but I bet you make them work pretty hard for you, don't you?*

Think about what excuses you use and what results you would see if you got rid of all of them.

Who is responsible for the results that you get?

It's not the people around you, behind you, or in front of you, and it's certainly not this book—it's the person reading it. Every time you point your finger at someone or something else, remember there are three pointing back at you.

If you put all the ideas here into practice and achieved great results, would we have done that for you? No. You'd have done it for yourself. You can only blame yourself for your success.

Set yourself goals and take 100% responsibility for the results. Do not make someone else responsible for the results you see. If you have not achieved your goal yet, ask yourself, 'What excuses did I give myself?' Then set about doing it differently next time.

You are part of the problem

No need to be offended. I'm part of the problem too. You're creating your problems and I'm creating mine. The sooner we come to accept this very helpful fact, the sooner we can set about sorting out all the problems you think you have.

A problem is never really the whole problem; the part you play is the state in which you approach it. Everything you do is influenced by your state, and you've got more of those than the whole of America.

Romance is a state.
Happiness is a state.
Sadness is a state.

Anger is a state.
Joy is a state.
Depression is a state.
Shock is a state.
Anxiety is a state.
Excitement is a state.
Nervousness is a state.

I hope you're getting the picture...

States all happen on the inside. They don't need anything on the outside to happen in order to exist. You're perfectly skilled in creating states all by yourself. A blessing and a curse, right?

Let's give it a go. Close your eyes and remember a time when you felt slightly sad – not too sad; we don't want tears. Let's go for a five out of ten on the happy to sad scale.

What did you feel, say, hear, and see?

See the event through your own eyes so you cannot see yourself in the picture.

Feeling sad yet?

Now check out your physiology. How's that looking? *Are your shoulders back or slumped, are you sat up straight or hunched, are you smiling or frowning?*

Now, let's give happy a whirl. Put a great big smile across your face, even if it's a totally fake one. Punch the air, and say out loud, 'I am amazing, I'm so happy, I'm alive and it's going to be an awesome day.' If you're reading this in a public place and you choose to do this, I'm even more excited to ask this next question...

How are you feeling?
Liberated?
Embarrassed?
Happy?

Your state can totally change in just one second.

Choosing to accept that your state is in your control is a very powerful experience.

It means that you are no longer a victim of whatever events you experience. **You are the creator of your state.**

You are the creator

When anything happens on the planet, typically something caused it or created it in the first place.

You could decide to believe that everything in your life was 'caused' by you. The alternative is to believe that everything in your life was 'caused' by someone or something outside of you. And what you are experiencing is the 'effect'.

The ability to choose to be 'at cause' for events in your life is the most empowering mindset of all. Like most things, it has a dark and a light side.

If you are causing all the good stuff, you must also be causing all the shitty stuff too. Unfortunately, you can't agree with one and dismiss the other.

Which side of the equation are you on in your life?
Are you on the effect side of situations, circumstances, and other people?
Or are you the creator of things in your life?
*Are you willing to accept that **you** are the creator?*

Successful people tend to live on the cause side of the equation. When anything happens to them, they ask themselves, 'How did I create this?' and, 'What do I need to do to create things differently in the future?' They ask, *'What can I learn from this event that will allow me to create things I want next time?*

This is elite-level accountability and mental freedom.

How far do you take this?

That depends on what results you want. Every time something happens to you, ask yourself, 'How did I create this?'

You want to do this because if you are on the effect side of the equation, you are experiencing the creation of something by someone or something else. You have no control. You have limited choice. The good news is you will always have someone or something to blame!

If you are on the cause side of the equation of everything you are experiencing, that means you created it. So, if you accept this, you can influence it, and you have an abundance of choice.

Remember, we are not saying this is true. Things may happen that you did not 'cause'. By acting as if you did cause it, you can choose how to respond. *Ask yourself, 'How did I create this situation of not achieving my goal and what do I need to change to get a different result?'* Acting as if you are the cause of everything truly is empowerment, influence, and choice.

In my experience of coaching people living with cancer, I have often had people share with me that they had been unhappy with their job and with their life before their diagnosis. Since having cancer, they had made the decision to change their job, prioritise time with family, and that, for them, the whole experience had been a positive one. Did they 'cause' their cancer? Does it matter? By deciding to choose to act as if they had created it, they felt empowered to use it to change their lives.

I love living life at cause. Stuck in traffic, I probably created this so I could listen to my audiobook a bit longer. Losing the house I wanted to buy, I created this because the next house would be even better, and it was!

When you bring the problem inside of you, you also bring the solution inside of you. All the times you say the problem is outside of you, you are also saying the solution is outside of you too.

I choose to believe that everything that happens to me in my life is all me. This means I get to learn from the effect I want to stop creating and take full credit for all the good stuff I have created.

You are a projection of your own perception

Carl Jung was a famous Swiss psychiatrist and psychotherapist who founded the school of analytical psychology. He said that everything you perceive outside of you; situations, people, circumstances, events, etc., are all a projection from inside of you, and as soon as you become aware of it, it's you. All you have around you is your perception. There is no 'reality' just your perception. Remember, your very own atlas.

If you are creating your own reality, then why wouldn't you want it to be amazing?

Have you ever been about to meet someone and someone else says to you, 'Oh no! You're not meeting with *them*, are you? They're awful! You'll have a really difficult time.' Then when you turn up for the meeting you get on brilliantly. Afterwards, you speak to this person again and say, 'It went really well. We got on great,' and they say, 'It must have been a different person I was thinking of then.'

It wasn't two different people. It was two different perceptions and two different projections of the same person.

Has it ever happened the other way round for you? You have gone into a situation expecting it to be a nightmare, and guess what, it was! Was it them? Or was it your projection of your perception of them?

When we are in a bad mood the world seems to be pretty miserable, and we clash with our friends or colleagues or our family. When we are in a great mood, we notice the good stuff. We smile and strangers smile back, and we get better results.

Start noticing what you perceive of the people, events, and situations around you. Start thinking, if I'm projecting all this, how is this all me? This might be easier for the good things but not so easy for the bad things.

Most people think, 'It's out there,' and, 'It's them!' Successful people think, 'Okay, this is all me; this is my projection, this is my creation. What do I need to change inside of me so I will see the change outside of me?'

Think of two examples from your own life, one where you had a successful outcome and one where you felt like a failure. This can be in any context: work, sport, home, health.

Let's start with the failure.

Think about (maybe write down) a list of all of the factors that led to that failure.

Once you have done that, shake it off. Maybe stand up and sit down or make a cup of tea. Whatever it takes to shake off that 'state'.

Now let's take the successful outcome.

Again, make a list of all the factors that led to the successful outcome. Once you have done that, compare the two lists and see what you notice.

Firstly, is one list longer or are they the same?

Was it easier for you to find reasons/excuses for the failure than reasons for the success or the other way around?

Secondly, notice which factors were cause and which were effect. Cause will be all of the factors that were totally down to you, your attitude, skills, and behaviours. Effect will be all the factors that were outside of you, the weather, other people, luck, etc.

Notice for each event which list is longest.

Some people tend to blame themselves for failure, believing that they are at 'cause' for everything that goes wrong. And when they do experience success, they only notice the factors where they are at 'effect'. They say it was luck or it was because of someone else's help.

This means they can't even enjoy their success as they do not give themselves credit for it.

And, of course, some people do the reverse. They take credit for all their successes (at cause) and blame everyone and everything else for any failures (at effect).

Neither of these types is helpful. It is only by acknowledging how your actions contributed to both the success and the failure that you can learn and grow.

After any success or failure, look for both the cause factors and the effect factors.

Ask yourself what you did to make this a success or a failure. How can you repeat this or avoid this in the future? What is there to learn?

What external factors *(effect)* contributed to this success or failure? How can you repeat this in the future or avoid this? What is there to learn?

Just one more cold, hard truth… if you can handle it.

You are a shitty director (sometimes)

Movie directors have a great job. They get to take state-altering stories and bring them to life. Along with the team, they choose the actors, where they stand, how they speak, what they say. They get to choose the lighting, which cameras are used, the position and angle of each camera. They choose the music, the songs, what gets played and when. All this is done with the intent of creating an experience. They connect with our fears, desires, and necessities. They can make us feel romantic, happy, sad, angry, joyful, depressed, shocked, anxious, excited, nervous. The director of the movie has the power through their choices to alter our state.

You have the power to do this too. *Are you ready for it?*

You are the director of you. Everything you see, hear, and feel is being created by you.

You are a liar – until you accept you are the cause.

You are part of the problem – until you take ownership of your state.

You are the creator – of your own life.

You are a projection of your own perception – make sure you have positive projections.

You are a shitty director – but there's time to get much better.

Here is an activity that can profoundly change your behaviour.

Begin by identifying the behaviour you want to change.

You may want to change your behaviour around a particular food or habit:

eating chocolate, smoking, running, going to the gym, getting angry when you're late, drinking alcohol, getting up early, getting frustrated when the house is a mess, whatever it is that you would like to change.

When you think about (insert behaviour you would like to change here), do you have a picture?

Ask yourself these questions to identify all the qualities of the picture. It might help to write down your answers, or you could get someone else to ask you the questions and note down your answers.

Visual

Is it black and white or colour?
Is it a movie or a still?
Is the picture big or small?
Is it near or far?
Where is it located? (e.g. top left or right?)

Is it bright or dim?
Anything else you notice about the picture?

Auditory

Are there any sounds that are important?
Are they loud or soft?
Anything else you notice about the sound?

Kinaesthetic

Are there any feelings that are important?
Is it heavy or light?
Where is it located?
Size?
Pressure?
Vibration?
Anything else you notice about the feeling?

Once you have identified all the qualities, now the fun can begin.

You're the director. *What happens when you change them?*

If it is black and white, change it to colour. If it is a movie, change it to a still. Move the location of the picture. Make it smaller and further away or bigger and nearer.

How does this change how you experience the belief about that behaviour? You may well find that it totally changes how you perceive that belief. It may even disappear completely.

Prisha's Story

Prisha is thirty-six, divorced, a mother of two kids aged fourteen and twelve, and works full time. There never seem to be enough hours in the day. She is constantly juggling and feels like she is constantly failing. Her relationship with her ex is stressful. He often misses planned visits and cancels at the last minute when he is supposed to have the kids for a weekend.

Lockdown had only added to the mix, with working from home and home-schooling. She said, 'My life is a mess. I'm busy all of the time. The house is a state, the kids do nothing to help, and no one listens to me.'

Prisha attended one of our group coaching workshops we offered during lockdown. The group met for two hours at a time, once a fortnight, for six sessions.

In week one, Prisha joined the Zoom call and had fairly low expectations of the programme.

We started by explaining how the six sessions would work together and that, by the end of the programme, they would have the tools to create a new life story. Prisha was sceptical. During the discussions she would look for opportunities to disagree and dispute what we suggested: 'You say I could just change my perception but that's not going to make my house tidy or get my ex to pick the kids up on time.'

By the second session we had shared some of the cold, hard truths and the group was gradually accepting that the problem was them, not the outside world. Prisha was devastated.

She said, 'So, along with all the other shit, you're telling me that I am doing this to myself. That this is all my fault. That I could just change it if I wanted to. She was near to tears by this point.

It was tough to watch, and yet we knew this was the process. Without acknowledging responsibility and ownership she would continue to be powerless to change.

Then the tide started to turn. She realised that we weren't saying she was to blame, and yet we were saying the only person who could change it was her. She had to decide that this was no longer acceptable. It was her attitude that had to change. She could decide to be okay with the messy house or she could decide to stop settling for it.

And then she surprised us all. She said, 'I'm going to call a family meeting. I'm going to tell the kids that I need them to help. I need them to start putting their own things away and doing the washing up.'

We explored how she could use the same techniques with the kids that we had used with her. Give them responsibility. Ask them how they like living like this, what do they want to change, and how can they help?

The following session we waited to hear how she had got on. She seemed like a totally different person. 'I can't believe this has worked, 'she said. 'I just decided that I was not going to put up with this anymore.'

Instead of walking into a messy room where the kids were watching TV, sighing and rolling her eyes and getting frustrated and tidying it herself, she now asks the kids to switch the TV off for ten minutes and tidy up.

She has also changed her attitude to her ex, accepting that he cannot be relied on, and refusing to let his behaviour make her feel worthless.

Choosing your own life story starts by accepting that you are the one with the power and the responsibility.

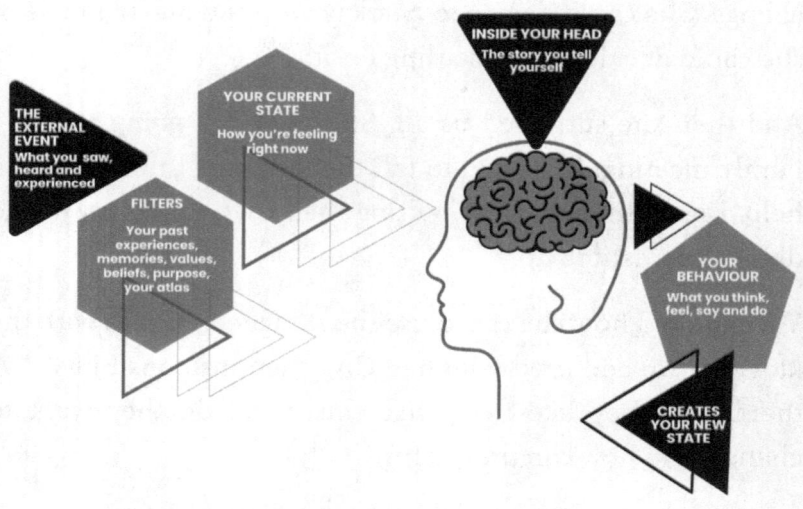

Human Filtering Process

5

BEYOND THE BULLSHIT
YOU CHOOSE TO BELIEVE YOU ARE THE STORY MASTER

Karl Pilkington is known for being a straight talker. I like him. A quick search online and you'll find an array of short clips and memes of him saying BULLSHIT in moments when he believes someone is telling him a fanciful or exaggerated story. Imagine having one of these incredible inventions in life, an unfiltered shortcut button that announces what you're really thinking. It may result in getting fired now and then, and a few unnecessary arguments, but wouldn't it feel amazing?

You sit in a meeting and someone is clearly making something up – press the button and the voice of Karl Pilkington shouting BULLSHIT echoes around the room.

Your child tells you a story about why they got detention at school – BULLSHIT.

You tell yourself some cock and bull story about why you can't work out today – BULLSHIT.

You tell yourself you're 'not good enough' or 'smart enough' - BULLSHIT.

This chapter contains a load of cock and bull stories that we have either believed for years or tell ourselves every day. There is always something beyond the bullshit.

Kay's Story - Christmas 1987

It was just a normal, average Christmas all around—below average if I were to compare it to other Christmases, in fact. However, I'm not comparing it to other Christmases, I'm comparing it to nothing at all. I'm thinking of one particular moment that lasted less than five seconds yet filled my future Christmases with joy and excitement.

Have you ever had a moment like that? A moment when something happens that lasts seconds yet stays with you for hours, weeks, years, sometimes a lifetime?

The mill town where I was born and bred supported itself through traditional trades, and both my parents worked in a woven fabrics factory. Every year, the company held an awesome Christmas party for their employees' children at the cricket club. My big brother and I looked forward to it so much! We got amazing presents which we were allowed to open, even though it was weeks before Christmas Day.

That's the magic of being a child, especially at Christmas. We absorb the excitement, and when we are told that this guy in a red suit who lives at the North Pole spends all year making toys with his magic elves to deliver to all the children in the whole world in just one night, we believe it.

Mid-party, without warning, the music stopped and the big light went on, revealing a room of sweaty, confused, and light-dazzled kids trying to work out who had interrupted their annual rave. The adults shushed us to listen. Silence fell. Frozen in that quiet, we listened intently. Our full awareness was still, we were in the moment with no idea what we were supposed to hear, to just listen and notice.

We all became aware simultaneously of bells chiming from the dark sky outside. The room erupted into nervous, excited laughter.

Mum ushered us out of the club. I had barely stepped out the door, and my eyes attached themselves to the star-filled winter sky with magnetic force. Gazing upward, I saw him in full three-dimensional, high-definition vision (the human eye being far more advanced than technology could muster in the 80s). There he was, sitting proudly in his magnificent sleigh, complete with reindeer and lights as bright as beacons as he shot through the sky at the speed of light.

The real Santa was flying through the sky! I'm not making this up; seriously, he was! I see him now with the same clarity as I saw him then. Even now as a fully grown adult I can still look up to the sky on a cold, dark winter's night, notice the stars glistening, and feel those feelings with the same intensity as I did then.

The bells carried on the wind, followed by the deeper tones of Santa's voice calling, 'Ho, ho, ho!' The hot spice of the adults' mulled wine travelled up my nose as they warmed their hands on their cups.

I easily recall the joy and happiness glowing like a warm ball of fire inside my chest. The world stood still for a moment that night. My jaw dropped as what I could see, hear, and feel integrated inside my mind. Any slight doubt I may have had vanished completely—Santa is real!

Leaving the party that night, I was not the same as I was when I walked in. I had my new toy in hand and a newly reinforced belief that the big man was real.

Santa is real. Full stop.

My parents had 'slip ups' many times after that day, but whilst the adults were hushing and shushing as they discussed matters not for my ears in the run up to the twenty-fifth of December, the shift in my belief system about Santa being real had already been successful in blocking anything to the contrary out. That belief was well and truly locked in.

As children, and even as adults, we build an internal world we can understand, a world we want. We grasp hold of those things that back up our beliefs, even when logic and reason could burst the bubble if we look closely enough. I wanted to believe. I was given proof, and I was happy to accept it, even when given clues to the contrary.

Jacqui's Story - I Hate Sundays

Well, I used to. I used to spend the whole day on Sunday dreading Monday. If I was travelling to a different city to deliver a training course, I was an expert in working myself up into a state over it.

It meant that my weekend was destroyed by over-thinking what was going to happen on Monday.

I'd start by imagining all the things that could go wrong, starting with not waking up on time. What if my alarm clock didn't go off? I set two, one on my bedside clock, one on my phone. Then I'd focus on packing everything, and I mean everything! Mary Poppins had nothing on my kit bag. You name it, I packed it. Pens, spare pens, extra pens, marker pens and whiteboard pens: that sounds like enough for the pens. Now on to post it notes.

But the universe still had lots of other tricks up its sleeve that could derail my day. What if my sat nav failed and I found myself in the middle of nowhere? Or what if there was a traffic jam on the motorway? That would be just my luck.

Once I'd got myself all nicely anxious about simply getting there, I would turn my attention to setting up for the session. Maybe my laptop wouldn't work or there wouldn't be a projector, or I'd forget the handouts. Last but not least, I would work myself up about the event itself. Maybe the delegates wouldn't like me, or they didn't want to be there, or they already knew more about the subject than me. By then I could be in a complete state of anxiety and worry and I believed that anything that could go wrong would. It was exhausting.

What had to change? What made a massive change to my life and got my Sundays back? I told myself a different story.

Since it was only a story – I had no means of telling the future and predicting what was going to happen – I decided to tell myself a different one. In this new story I woke up on time, popped my stuff in the car, arrived at my destination on time and the whole event was a great success.

Lisa's Story

Lisa is an athlete who has experienced more than her fair share of injury. She was not performing her best when she returned to her sport, so she contacted me for some advice.

Prior to her accident she was at the top of her game. She had secured a space on an international team which came with full sponsorship. She was seen as the most experienced person on the team, the one the others looked up to and wanted to be like.

She took the time she needed to heal her injury and got back as soon as physically possible. However, on returning to her sport she didn't feel the same.

She said, 'I'm so concerned about getting injured again. I can't afford to have any more time off. I'll get too far behind and everyone else in my class is already doing better than me. I need to catch up.'

I asked, 'How are you doing that?'

She was panicking and visibly distressed. 'I've been spending double the amount of the time in the gym, working hard, and I've stopped seeing my friends. I'm putting everything in but it's not working.'

'Tell me how you were before the injury,' I said.

She was able to reply immediately. 'I was so confident,' she said. 'I didn't think about injury or what anyone else was doing. I just did my thing. I loved it.'

We identified that she used to be relaxed, and that when she was relaxed she was able to just focus on having fun. She didn't think about anything.

I asked her how it might be if we put some fun things into her schedule outside of her sport. Lisa agreed that she would like that, but she was concerned that she was getting behind.

'Is what you are doing now helping you relax?' I asked.

'Not at all,' she said. 'The more I try and perform better, the worse I am getting.'

Lisa agreed that we could make a new plan for the next month and see what happened.

Lisa began to realise that she wasn't using a recipe for success, that she was doing all the things that stopped her from being at her best and which created the problem. She had told herself a story that she must stay injury free because she couldn't afford any more time away from her sport.

We changed that narrative to one in which Lisa had to relax because when she relaxed she performed better and was less likely to get injured.

We changed Lisa's narrative from telling herself she needed to work doubly hard to catch up to telling herself to make sure she was having fun in and outside of her sport because when she did, she relaxed and performed better.

We changed the narrative from, 'I'm not where I should be,' to, 'I'm exactly where I'm meant to be right now.'

Lisa went to her next event eight days later and took 25% off her previous competition time.

Kay's Story - Taking Control

The warm, prickling sensation ran over my skin. Could I make it in time? Yes, thank god. Wow, that was close. The stomach cramps were excruciating, the cold sweats were chilling, but now I was feeling much better and the pain was starting to subside, at least for now.

It was getting cold in there and I could hear people outside. There was a queue forming, but I couldn't come out just yet ...

My habit had grown. It was taking over at work as well as at home.

This was how I had learned to deal with my life. This was my toxic and embarrassing secret. My saviour was laxatives. I was taking them by the truck load. This was the fourth time I'd visited the porcelain god that day. It didn't start with taking many of them.

I remember the day it started. I finished my shift at my Saturday job in town and got my day's wages – seven pounds and fifty pence, to be precise.

I'd already decided the previous week what this money would be spent on. I was going into the local health shop. Sounds ideal, right? It seems ironic looking back that the very thing that destroyed my health was bought in a health food shop. I stood outside feeling super nervous, like I was hanging around on a street corner waiting for the dealer to arrive with my next fix.

I walked into the shop and picked up the biggest bottle of laxatives on the shelf. If you're going in, you might as well go in big, I say. I approached the counter with my prepared speech: they weren't for me, my mum had sent me for them. She wasn't well and couldn't make it herself. To my surprise, the checkout girl didn't even look at what I was about to purchase, she simply popped the pills in a bag, took my money and said goodbye – the deal was done.

Buying these pills was my totally fucked-up way of thinking I was taking control of my life. I was in charge now. I couldn't control anything else, but I could control this – yes, yes, yes. I felt good about this decision, I was a grown up and I was in charge of what happened in my life.

When I got home, I ran upstairs to my bedroom, carefully closed the door and checked no one was around before taking that big arse bottle of life-changing pills out of my bag and hiding them right at the back of my wardrobe where nobody would ever find them. Like I said, I was totally in control, right?

I believe doing what I did then would today be labelled as an eating disorder of some sort. Back then it didn't have a name that I might have read on the internet or heard on the TV. Google wasn't a thing so I had no idea it might be something other people could be doing too. It was just something I had decided to do for me.

I started taking one every night before bed. Within a few years I had increased this to four a night. They stopped having the same effect eventually so the only way to get that feeling of relief was to take more pills. The more I took, the more my body seemed to get used to them.

By the time I was eighteen I was taking up to ten a night and weighed just under seven stone. My weight had dropped to such a degree that people had begun to notice. I had gone from being 'lovely and slim' to looking malnutritioned and ill.

In an effort to hide the truth, I told lies, anything I could say to distract people from thinking it could be anything of concern. I decided to tell people I had an overactive thyroid and no matter what I ate the weight just dropped off – the envy of all my friends!

Although part of me knew what I was doing was making me ill, another more dominant part wanted to feel in control of my life and had told itself a story that this was how I would gain control of an otherwise spiralling world.

When I changed the story, I changed the way I felt, which led to taking a new action. That action was to stop taking the tablets. I chose to speak to a sports nutritionist and to learn about my body instead. He taught me about different foods, digestion, exercise and muscle groups. It was fascinating. I was still taking control; this time through positive action and making healthy choices for my mind and body.

Jacqui's Story – Okay, But Not Good Enough

I worked hard at school. I had to, and it was an effort. I wanted to do well, and it did not come easily. My younger brother, on the other hand, seemed to sail through. It appeared to be effortless to him. He would bring home spelling lists to learn and dismiss them as 'stupid'. He didn't have to try, and I tried all the time.

When I was about twelve years old and he was nine, we stayed at our Nan and Grandad's for a holiday. I loved my Nan. We had a very special relationship. I was born on her birthday, so I was her 'birthday present'. One particular day we were out shopping and my Nan ran into one of her friends and didn't pass up the opportunity to show off her grandchildren. She said, 'This is my granddaughter, Jacqui; she does very well at school. This is my grandson, Michael; he is exceptional.'

I remember taking this in, deep into my heart. I told myself, 'Now I know where I stand. I'm good, but not exceptional. I can do that. I can be that.'

I carried it with me for years after. I didn't consciously know that I had until I started to learn about how my mind works. I was asked to think about the beliefs I was holding onto that weren't useful to me, and this hit me like a baseball bat to the brain.

I looked back over my life and considered whether I could see the impact of living my life through this lens. And I could. I could see the acceptance of not aiming too high, the utter surprise if the popular people wanted to be my friends.

My wonderful Nan would be devastated to hear this story. And I want to be clear, I know for absolute certainty that what she said was spoken with pride and love for both me and my brother.

Sometimes it's not the stories we tell ourselves, they are gifted to us by those we love.

Here's the thing...

We tell ourselves stories all the time. It's all we have. We never know all the information, so we fill the gaps with things we've made up.

> When we don't know the whole story, we fill the gaps with bullshit.

These stories become beliefs as we forget they are stories and behave as if they are true. Some beliefs are helpful and empowering; others are limiting and make us miserable.

Santa, of course, is a useful belief that brings joy and happiness at Christmas time.

Taking those pills meant having control, except that of course they did not. It was not a useful belief. It was a limiting belief, a belief that limited choice, health, and the ability to be happy.

Spending all day Sunday believing that Monday was going to be dreadful may have been an attempt to feel prepared for every worst-case scenario, but instead it just caused stress and worry.

We all have lots of beliefs that we hold to be true about ourselves and the world around us.

Many of these beliefs are really empowering and useful, such as, 'I'm a good friend,' or, 'It's dangerous to cross the road without looking left, right and left again.'

But some of our beliefs are limiting beliefs. They stop us doing things, they hold us back, and they limit our behaviour and our potential. They are often based on little or no data and sometimes on other people's data.

Most of our phobias are beliefs we have learnt from the people around us when we are young. If you see your mum scream when she sees a spider, you immediately believe that spiders are scary and that screaming is the appropriate response.

Beliefs keep us safe. It's how we learn not to put our fingers in the fire. Maybe that spider was deadly.

It's also where all *-isms* come from: sexism, racism, ageism and so on. Discrimination is a story we tell ourselves about a group of people. What 'beliefs' do you have about 'young people', 'old people', 'football supporters' or 'millionaires'?

We are not able to predict the future or read people's minds. We simply make up stories and those stories change the way we feel and therefore behave. Why then do we seem to choose to make up the disaster version?

You may well have said the phrase, 'I know what you're thinking.' And of course, we know it isn't true, we are just making assumptions. How often have you worried that you have upset someone because they haven't called you in a while, only to discover that they have been dealing with something that you had no idea about?

It isn't just people. We can tell ourselves that the traffic jam when we are running late, or the rain on the day of our picnic, is being done to us, as if the universe is conspiring to ruin our day.

Some of it is self-protection. We think that if we imagine all the things that can go wrong, we will somehow be better prepared for it when it happens. We also love to be proved right. So, if I tell myself it will go wrong, I can smugly say, 'I told you so' if it does. If it doesn't go wrong, I can dismiss it as dumb luck.

How do you start to reframe the story? How do you look for the positive possibility or simply accept that you don't know what will happen?

That rain on the day of your picnic isn't doing it to you to spoil your day. It is a natural process that has nothing to do with you. You could make the decision to move your picnic indoors and have a fabulous time because of, not despite, the rain.

The person who hasn't called you may have things going on in their life that you know nothing about. And that traffic jam on the motorway might have made you late, which just might have put you in exactly the right spot at the right time. There are lots of stories of people who should have been in the World Trade Center in New York on September eleventh 2001, but something happened that made them late or made them change their plans at the last minute and this ended up saving their life.

The story I'm telling myself

We love the phrase, 'The story I'm telling myself is...'

It reminds us instantly that that is all it is, a story. We have the facts from our point of view, our own perspective, our own atlas.

All the cold, hard truths we have shared with you, and all the gritty attitudes, they are all stories too.

If we are going to tell ourselves stories all the time, then tell helpful, useful, empowering stories? Stories that give us choice, opportunities and courage rather than stories that diminish us and make us scared to even try.

By choosing to believe the useful beliefs and adopting the gritty attitudes, you will have the choice to choose the life you want and stop telling yourself lies.

You will grow your grittitude.

What stories do you tell yourself every day? Are they helpful or do they make you an anxious mess?

Start to notice and challenge your thinking. It's helpful to actually say the phrase, 'The story I'm telling myself is...'

What story do you want to tell instead?

How will your life be better when you change the current story you're telling yourself?

What if all it took to change the story was to challenge it?

The questions below will help you challenge the belief and change the story. They will take you beyond the bullshit.

Some of them are not rational as we are not dealing with a rational thought process. And we are not talking to our rational, conscious mind, we are talking to our unconscious mind.

How do you know this story was true?

What examples do you have of when it isn't true?

What examples do you have of when it is both true and untrue?

When is it neither true nor untrue?

How do you know this belief is untrue when you think about it now?

What do you want to believe instead?

How do you know that this new belief is already true?

Now check in. How are you feeling about the belief now? Is it starting to lose credibility? If it now seems less convincing but still somewhat true, then run the process again. You are aiming for the limiting story to totally disappear and to replace it with a useful, empowering one.

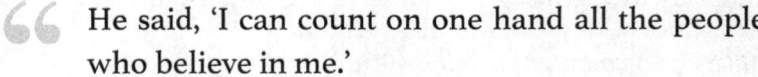

> He said, 'I can count on one hand all the people who believe in me.'
>
> I said, 'I can count on one finger the only one that matters.'
>
> Believe in you.

6

HERE'S THE THING

YOU CHOOSE TO BELIEVE ALL BEHAVIOUR HAS A POSITIVE INTENTION

Simone's Story

Simone was referred to me for coaching by Macmillan. She had been diagnosed with cancer a little over a year before. Her chemotherapy was coming to an end, and she wanted to start to make plans for returning to work and normal life.

In our first session she shared that she didn't want to go back to how things were before the cancer. She no longer wanted her job to be all consuming and stressful.

I asked her if she wanted a new job or a different attitude to her old one. This made her pause; she hadn't considered that both were an option.

We explored what she enjoyed about her current job and what would have to change to make her happy to go back.

She said, 'I think I'd have to get better at saying no and being okay with not always being the one to volunteer every time a new challenge comes up.'

I asked what she wanted instead. She said, 'I want to be able to give my all while I am at work, and then, when my day is finished, switch off and really be present for my family and start to do all the fun things I have always promised my kids that we will do together.'

I asked her how she felt when she was taking on every extra challenge and working late into the evenings and weekends. She confessed that a part of her enjoyed the feeling that she was important and that people relied on her to get things done. We talked about how she felt on a Sunday morning when she had to say to her kids that mummy just had to send a few emails.

'I can't win,' she said. 'I want to do a good job and I want to be there for my kids. I don't see how I can do both!'

I asked Simone to name one thing she could change that would make a difference. She thought about it for a minute and then smiled, and I could see her body language change. She sat up straighter, her chin went up and she had more energy. She explained that there was a project she was struggling with that was really taking more time than she had expected, and one of her direct reports had been hinting that she would like to get more involved. She started to weigh up the possibility of handing responsibility of the whole thing to them.

We discussed what she would need to put in place to help her direct report be successful and feel supported. I also asked how she would feel if they approached the task in a different way to her. What would stop her from stepping in and taking over?

She said that she knew it would be a challenge, but she knew it was the right thing to do. Since having cancer, she no longer wanted her entire life to be about being successful at work.

She said she was going to book tickets for Sunday to take her kids to the zoo.

Why do we do things that we know are bad for us?

We know that tobacco, alcohol, and sugar are bad for us, especially if we really go for them in large quantities. You may well have woken up the next morning asking yourself why you overindulged. The question may arise when you stand on the scales or attempt to go for a run.

The reason we do these things is because there is always something to be gained from them.

Maybe you feel happy, stressed, fed up, or excited – in fact, any mood you can think of, and you hear that little voice in your head say, 'Hey, friend, let's get some of that stuff that makes you feel even happier, or calm, or rewarded…'

 "All behaviour has a positive intention"

Yes, you read that right. All behaviour has a positive intention. Remember, these are useful gritty attitudes to choose to live by. We didn't say they were always true.

You are behaving in a way that looks like it couldn't possibly be positive and yet, it must give you something or you wouldn't do it. It's also called 'secondary gain'. Once you understand what the positive intention of your behaviour is, you may be able to find a different behaviour that will give you the same outcome.

Try it out. Think of the things you say and do that you may not think have a positive intention and then challenge yourself to identify whether you do gain something after all. When we can't think of the gain immediately, it could be because we are not particularly proud of it or don't want to admit to it.

Have you ever said, 'I feel so fat. I look so horrible'? Maybe it's because you hoped someone would say, 'No, you don't, you look lovely.' Your secondary gain, in this case, was a compliment or reassurance.

Perhaps you say to yourself, 'I don't care if I don't get that job,' so that if you don't get it you can say to yourself, 'See, I was right. Nothing good happens to me.' The gain could be to protect yourself from feeling that you have failed, by having in fact proved yourself right.

Have you said yes to taking on extra work when you knew you didn't have the time because you like the secondary gain of feeling important, needed and indispensable?

When you have figured out what your positive intention is, or what the secondary gain is, you can find a better way of getting it. If your purpose is to calm yourself, you could take a walk or a bath instead of having a drink. You could simply ask someone how you look rather than complaining about looking fat in the hope they will disagree.

The impact of your behaviour will also be dependent on the context.

For example, an unwillingness to change your mind could mean you are being 'inflexible' in one meeting and 'single-minded' in another. Changing the context can change the meaning.

If someone says, 'I can never speak up in meetings,' you could say, 'It must be great to be able to reflect, rather than just leaping in with your point of view.'

Your challenge is when you find yourself behaving in a way that you think isn't positive. At those times, ask yourself, *'What is the purpose of this behaviour? What does it give me? Could I get the same thing by behaving in another way?'*

Also ask, *'Is this behaviour positive in another context?'*

And here's the kicker: if you struggle to find the positive intention of some of your behaviour, then it is near impossible to figure out the positive intention of someone else's. Next time someone says or does something that drives you crazy, upsets you or doesn't make any sense, remember there was a positive intention... but they might not know or understand what it was either.

Sometimes it's really subtle. Have you ever 'forgotten' to pack your trainers when you went on holiday, so you 'can't' go for a run? Have you 'forgotten' to take your PE kit to school, 'forgotten' your wallet on a date?

That act of self-sabotage may have been a genuine accident, possibly a happy accident, or maybe a downright intentional act to get the result you wanted.

By being more honest with yourself you can identify your real intention. Would it have felt different if you had made the conscious choice that on your weekend away you were going to relax and not go for a run, rather than 'tricking' yourself into getting the result you wanted?

What behaviours do you want to change?

What is the positive intention or secondary gain from this behaviour?

Ok, try again, really.

What purpose is this behaviour serving you?

How could you get this need met with a different behaviour?

How will your life improve if you choose to believe that there is a positive intention behind everyone else's behaviour?

It's not only about how you manage success. It's about how you manage failure.

One day you'll die.

7
ONE DAY YOU'LL DIE
SORRY NOT SORRY

We live each day as though we have no time and yet live our lives as though we'll never run out.

Most people do not get advance notice of their death, no red letter, no snooze button, no final warning.

If death were to knock on your door tomorrow, would you be ready, or would you look back and wonder why you wasted so much time?

No one will care if you were fat or thin, if you kept your house tidy or if you had lots of money.

What if you made the decision to live without waiting for death to be imminent?

The waiting is over. Be here, now. You have a choice.

Live.

Never look back, unless
it's to see
how far you have come.

PART 2

THE MESSY BIT IN THE MIDDLE

Go on then, take a look back.

Are you feeling proud, confident and intrepid or are you wishing you were back where you were before you began?

The map you started out with has already changed. Your world has expanded. The possibility for your story to go in new directions that you had never even noticed before is now within your reach. It's at this point of the adventure that the end may not yet be in sight, and neither is the beginning. You're in it now, and your perception has been changed forever.

You are not the person you were, and you can choose the person you want to be. In this final part, we share the secrets to keeping going when it gets tough.

Are you ready to follow the white rabbit further?

8

FEELS LIKE HEAVEN
YOU CHOOSE TO BELIEVE IN THE POWER OF PURPOSE

> "Our purpose is to fulfil your life, give you joy and unconditional love, to save you from yourself"
>
> *WOODY AND JESS THE LABRADOODLES*

They love us unconditionally even when we leave them in the house all day, forget to walk them or haven't made time to play ball. No matter what's happened that day they are always happy to see us and best of all they don't answer back. They ask for little, just companionship. It's easy to provide them with all the things they need.

For us less furry folk, finding our purpose in life can be a bit more challenging. When I pose the question, 'Why do you do what you do?' it's often met with still, blank and slightly fearful faces. It's a big question when you have never been asked it before.

We are pretty simple beings with very simple basic needs. I have yet to see a purpose statement that doesn't take us back to the rawest, simplest form of our human nature. Yet we make everything so complex. If you surface your true purpose in this mad, crazy world it makes the hard stuff feel much easier.

Jacqui's Story – My Idea of Heaven

When I was ten years old, I wanted to be a ballerina.

This wasn't exactly supported by my mum and dad. Dad couldn't get his head around why I would want to do this. He suggested tap dancing. He could at least see the appeal of that, but not ballet. They bought me a tutu to 'flounce round the house in' thinking this would satisfy the need, but all it did was make me want it more. Finally, I saw an advert pinned to the notice board in our local newsagent advertising ballet classes at our local youth centre. I was in. I loved it. That year we put on a show at the theatre. I remember so clearly the feeling of being backstage putting on costumes and make-up, then the performance and finally going back to take our bow.

The performance was Cinderella, and I was one of the horses pulling the carriage, with a pampas grass plume clamped to my forehead with tape and elastic. I couldn't have felt prouder if I had been in the leading role.

I was in heaven.

At twenty I was lucky enough to discover the job that I would love doing for the rest of my life, that of People Development.

I trained new joiners starting their careers with the organisation I worked for, and I loved it. I stood at the front of a room, explaining complex things in a way that made it easy for them to understand.

I was in heaven.

I started to go to Jazzercise, which is an aerobic dance fitness programme. I loved it. I loved learning the routines and being part of a group of people dancing for fun and fitness. I really wanted to become an instructor. I even led a few classes.

I was in heaven.

At thirty I was married to the love of my life, living in London, travelling all over the world delivering training across the global organisation.

I was in heaven.

At forty I found that there was a Jazzercise class nearby. From the very first night, I loved it again and told the instructor that I'd love to train to become an instructor myself. She said she'd help me and I could apply to start whenever I wanted.

I qualified within a few months. The feeling of standing on the stage, wearing my headset mic, and teaching a class to dance and have fun felt like the perfect merger between my early life of ballet and my work life as a trainer.

I was in heaven.

At fifty I am living my new dream life. I live with my wonderful husband and three boisterous cats in a house with a fabulous sea view. I have qualified as a professional coach, and I am writing a book with my best friend.

I am in heaven.

Here's the thing...

When you find your purpose, you find your passion.

I love that I love my job. It hasn't always been very well paid and that was never as important to me as being happy.

Identifying your life purpose is one of the most meaningful and powerful experiences you can have. It is the secret to unlocking your motivation and sense of satisfaction.

So, when you are feeling down, low in motivation or just a little lost with where you are right now, don't question everything, just ask the right questions about the few things that really matter...

Let's start with values.

Your values

Values are the things that are important to you.

Our values are created by our upbringing, parents, school, beliefs and experiences.

Until relatively recently it was believed that our values were in place by about age seven and after that they did not change. We now know that is not true. Our brains are very 'plastic'. They change and respond to new experiences.

When people have their first baby they will often say, 'Everything that was important to me suddenly changed.' They are describing a value shift. Trust me, if you've had one, you will know!

Fallen in love?

Had a child?

Lost someone you love?

Broken up from a relationship?

Experienced trauma?

If you are saying yes to any of these, you know exactly what I mean when I say you've had a 'value shift'. Something just feels different.

To identify your values ask yourself, *'What is important to me?'*

Write down all the words that come to you.

When you think you have run out of words, wait a few minutes and you will probably find yourself thinking of more. You may think these last-minute thoughts will be less important but the opposite is often true. Often, the words that come to us last are the most important ones.

Once you have a list, narrow it down to your top three.

You can have as many values as you want. The point of narrowing it down to the top three is to help you to identify what is really, *really* important to you.

To help you narrow them down, you could ask yourself, 'If I could have this but not that, would that be ok?' For example, if you have listed freedom and recognition as important, ask yourself, 'If I had loads of freedom but never got any recognition, would that be ok?' Also ask it in reverse: 'If I got loads of recognition but had no freedom, would that be ok?'

This way, you can decide if they are equally important or if one is more important than another. Remember, you can have all of your values, as many as you want: we just want to help you identify the ones that are most important to you.

You can do this for each context of your life. Maybe start by keeping it broad.

Start with the question of what's important to you. Then move on to asking what's important to you about your job, family, health, relationship, and so on.

You may find that a very different list emerges in each category, and may find a lot of similarities, especially in your top three in each category. The things that are most important to you will often be constant in all areas of your life.

Our values are connected to our motivations. We are motivated to do the things that are important to us. This answers a lot of questions, such as why some people wander into work late whilst others would be mortified at the thought of not being early.

Values influence your unconscious attention, that is, the things you pay attention to. They also influence your intentions, what you set out to achieve, your perceptions and judgements about what is good or bad, right or wrong, and your behaviour – so, why you do what you do. Values are the unconscious criteria that lead us to choose one thing over another.

Next time you say you haven't had time to do something, just know that that is not true. You haven't prioritised doing that thing because it's not as important to you as the thing you did do.

Even *where* you spend your time is a choice. It is an unconsciously directed choice but a choice, nevertheless.

Dan's Story

Dan has worked in the corporate environment for over twenty years. He has always been driven to do a great job and worked really hard to become a director in the company he works for. Over the last three years, he started to explore spirituality and religion and found it really helped him to stay calm and manage his emotions. This led to a deeper spiritual journey than he could ever have anticipated.

Whilst Dan has found this incredibly helpful, it has also led him to question his role at work, and his motivation towards it has dwindled.

I asked him to tell me what was really important in his life right now. Together we explored words and feelings until we were left with three words:

fun, freedom and connection.

These high-level intentions for his life are the guiding light to what makes him tick. When those three things are fulfilled he feels happy.

I asked Dan what he wanted to contribute to the world. After a few moments thought he said, 'To create a safe space.'

I asked him why. His answer was so that people were able to step into their own magic.

I repeated this back to him... 'You want to create a safe space so people are able to step into their own magic.'

Dan went quiet for a few moments. Tears filled his eyes, and he nodded with the realisation that this was his purpose. When he was doing things that aligned to this, he was happy.

When I asked if he was getting this from his work, he replied, 'No, not at all. Now it makes sense why I have been feeling so low and de-motivated.'

Over the coming days and weeks, we worked out a new plan that allowed him to find a new story for how he wanted to live his life now. It led to a new role working in health and wellbeing as well as some new hobbies that aligned to his purpose.

Surface your purpose

Now you've decided on your top three values, you can put them on one of those wooden signs and hang it in your home as a reminder of what's important to you. Plus, now your top three values are clear they will help you identify your purpose.

 "Your purpose is why you do what you do"

If your purpose is to support your family so they can live a life of freedom, you could do a job you didn't like because ultimately it helps you meet your purpose.

If your purpose is to learn new skills so you can create innovative products, you will want to do the research and spend hours studying in the evenings after a day at work.

If your purpose is to achieve gold in the Olympics so you can be the best in your sport, getting up early and missing social events feels like a small compromise.

Your purpose is what makes you get up in the morning. Once you know what it is, it makes it easier to make life decisions as every decision either supports your purpose or it doesn't.

Your purpose may be clear from your top values. Another way to identify what drives you is to create your own version of the reflection I did at the start of this chapter. Identify the things that gave you a sense of joy and satisfaction when you were a young child, a teenager, a young adult, and so on. Then look for the common thread that runs through them.

You may well be surprised to find a more common theme than you've previously noticed.

Do I have to change the world?

It is very compelling when we hear stories of people who have dedicated their life's work to helping others. The problem with hearing about people who are working towards curing disease, ending child poverty, and solving climate change is that it can make us feel like we should all have a purpose as far-reaching.

Your purpose doesn't have to be worthy or self-sacrificing. Your purpose is your purpose. If it drives you to take action, feels motivating and makes you feel fulfilled, then that is all that matters.

Motivation can be triggered from the inside and the outside.

Sure, we do some things because we enjoy them. We get a strong sense of achievement and would happily do them for no financial reward. The fire comes from inside you. This is the sort of motivation that makes you love going to work and to the gym. It's driven by your purpose; it's your passion.

When you do something because you feel you have to, the drive comes from outside of you. It could be to get paid or to make someone else happy, to buy a new car or a bigger house. This is the sort of motivation that makes you go to work even if you hate your job.

It's still driven by your purpose. If your purpose is security, this is what will make you get out of bed in the morning.

Your purpose may be something that is hard or even impossible to measure, different from a goal. If you set your purpose as being CEO of a company, you may not feel fulfilled until you achieve it, and then, if and when you do achieve it, it may not be what you hoped for. If your purpose is to be happy in your job, then you could experience that while trying to achieve your goal. If you get to CEO and it doesn't feel like you expected, you can find another goal while still experiencing the purpose of enjoying your job. Purpose is about the journey, not the end destination.

Purpose often does not have a definite end. Even ones like curing cancer and solving climate change may not have a definitive end point.

You may be very driven and have a purpose without knowing that's what it was called. You may not have learned about having a purpose, you are just driven toward your passion.

If you feel lost and empty and have no motivation, it might be because you have never taken the time to identify your purpose.

You may find that your passion and motivation have gone because your purpose is no longer being met. Maybe your life has changed, and you have not found a new purpose to drive you in this new chapter of your story.

For example, if a parent's purpose is their child's safety, security and happiness what happens when their child grows up and moves out or you lose connection completely?

What about the person totally driven by their career who gets made redundant, retires, or can no longer work for some reason?

When you understand that you feel loss and emptiness because your purpose is no longer being fulfilled, you can actively look for a new purpose, this can be all it takes to reignite the spark that makes you want to get out of bed in the morning.

If your values are not being met in one area of your life, it might be that they are being met in another.

I once had a client whose top values included excitement. I asked how much excitement he got in his job and he said none. But it turned out he was also a volunteer for the RNLI (Royal National Lifeboat Institute) and that provided plenty of excitement.

Grace's Story

A few years ago, I was coaching Grace, who worked in a corporate job and wanted to leave and start her own business.

She told me a bit about the plans, and I was struck that I wasn't hearing much passion or excitement for this new venture. I asked why she wanted to run her own business and she talked about earning more money. I asked if she would still start the business if she won the lottery on Saturday. She said no. I asked why not.

She said, 'Because I would then have the freedom to give up work and spend more time with my kids.'

This told me that the dream of the new business was not about money or a desire to do what the business involved, it was all driven by a desire to have more time to spend with her kids.

Once she realised what was important to her, it was much easier to make decisions. Could she stay in her corporate job and have more time with her kids? She could probably work fewer hours or negotiate more flexibility.

What if starting her own business turned out to be more time-consuming than she first thought?... As many new entrepreneurs discover! Then she would have even less time with her kids.

Figuring out what you want, and what you *really* want, not what you might think you want, is a crucial step to creating happiness.

What are your top three values?

What is your purpose?

To what extent are your values being met?

What do you need to change to get more of your values met?

How will knowing your purpose change your story?

9

DREAMS, GOALS AND BUCKETS
YOU CHOOSE TO BELIEVE YOU CAN

Jacqui's Story – A Ridiculous Challenge

I love a ridiculous challenge!

I get very motivated by new and seemingly unattainable goals, like climbing Ben Nevis, completing the London Marathon, and writing this book!

I know the goal is just the right amount of stretch when on one hand it feels completely bonkers and on the other hand it feels really exciting.

I remember the exact moment it was suggested that I do the London Marathon. I was going through one of my many weight-loss journeys, and I wanted to find a new incentive to get fitter. The minute the suggestion of the marathon was made, I got this excited feeling inside. A huge smile spread across my face and I said the words, 'That's ridiculous!' Simultaneously, my mind fast-forwarded to a clear image of me crossing the finish line and I knew that it would feel amazing to be able to say to myself, 'You did it, Jacqui; you have completed the London Marathon!'

In the same nanosecond, I slumped. Surely it was too huge? I mean, it's practically impossible to get a space... yet that image of me crossing the finish line popped up again, along with an intense feeling of satisfaction and pride.

I went home with these new waves of emotion washing through my mind and body. That evening I perched my laptop on my knees and started researching how to get a place in the London marathon. A number of links for various charities appeared. I then applied to six charities who, over the next few hours, all politely declined.

Some of the charities operated their own ballot system, and I couldn't even get a space to apply for a space. As the feeling of defeat began to creep over me, one of the smaller charities replied to say I had a space. This couldn't really be happening, I thought. They must mean I have a space in their ballot.

I replied to check: 'When you say I have a space, do you mean I have a space in your ballot, or could you possibly mean that I have a space in the actual marathon?'

A quick reply came back to confirm that yes, I had a space in the race, the actual event!

Within five hours of the crazy idea being put in my mind, I was in possession of a place in the 2016 London Marathon.

The training was a slog. At my lowest point, I stepped off a curb and was narrowly missed by a turning car. At that moment, I thought that if I got hit by a car, just a tiny bit, just enough to have to give this up, that would be okay. There were also a few bus rides home as I just stopped and refused to put one more foot in front of the other.

The day of the marathon arrived, and I powerwalked the whole thing with my arms pumping and a smile on my face. Turns out that wearing a t-shirt with your name on it in an event like that is very uplifting indeed!

Never trust dope

When setting a new goal, you get a great big shot of dopamine which makes you feel amazing, all fired up and ready to take on the world. It makes you feel braver and willing to try new things. You can't trust it entirely, though. That's the version of you riding the crest of a wave at the thought of this new and seemingly impossible challenge you have set yourself... but like any wave, it will come crashing down to shore. Then what?

Whilst the dope will get you fired up and ready to go, it can also make you feel a little crappy too. When it goes, you can be mentally tricked. You might think you have lost your passion, that it was a bad idea anyway or even feel silly for contemplating such a challenge.

That wasn't passion. It was your biology firing dopamine into you like a '90s raver popping ecstasy tablets. That moment wasn't and can't be an indicator of anything and especially not of passion. Passion for your goals is something that is developed and nurtured over time. There is no quick win so be patient. Let the dope flow when the idea comes and remember that's how it starts, but also remember that the really important part is what you do next.

Here's the thing...

I kept going, even when it was hard, because the motivation came from the inside.

Top-level athletes, successful business people, and high achievers in all fields have at least one thing in common: they all set goals and they stick with them, not just for days, or months, but sometimes years. Setting a goal gives you long-term vision. What may have previously seemed like a long and pointless grind becomes a positive pursuit in making your dreams become your reality.

Creating this level of focus helps you to organise your time and resources so that you can make the very most of YOUR time and YOUR life. There will be setbacks and obstacles along the way. There will be moments when you question why you started in the first place. Build those moments into the plan because I can 100% promise you, they will come.

Goal setting, when done properly, supports the process of making associations between what you want and what you currently have.

Sometimes part of you says, 'Go for it,' and the other part says, 'No, don't. It will never work out.' When those two parts of your mind battle with each other it can feel so exhausting that in the end, you give in to the path of least resistance, seduced by the voice in your head telling you it's okay to give up as you probably won't make it anyway. That voice will guide you back to the easier route, the one you have taken many times before.

You know the feeling, right?

I'm quite sure that path will be easier. It may even come without setbacks or obstacles, and it probably doesn't lead anywhere worth going!

You might notice yourself saying that part of you wants one thing and part of you wants another thing… this is your mind in conflict. It's the alignment of those two or more parts that will catapult you towards your deepest desires. You can start to connect 'the mind in conflict' by working out the highest level of positive intention between those different parts of your mind. Then you understand that they can join together in harmony, ultimately delivering the results you do really want.

Dreams, goals, and bucket lists

It is sometimes said that dreams are wishes, goals are plans. And while this may be true, there is something more magical about the word *dream* than *goal*.

You can call it what you like. All that matters is that you are working towards it, all the time.

As for bucket lists, the same applies. *Bucket list* suggests the goal is further away. Remember that you don't know how long you have. We've already pointed out that you will die one day, just as it will happen to us all. *Does your goal really have to wait until the end is in sight?*

Sure, some dreams are longer term. That trip that will deserve more than your four-week annual leave allowance; the house you want to buy isn't within your budget yet; your retirement plans will take a while.

Act as if your dream is a foregone conclusion. *If you knew for absolute certain that you would achieve your goal, is there something you would do today that would help to create it?*

Maybe you could do your research and find out the best time of year to make the trip, start learning the language, select one item that you could choose to go without in order to put that money away towards the dream. It is only by creating a pathway of individual steps between today and the goal that you will be able to keep walking towards it, every day.

Secondary gains

Remember that 'all behaviour has a positive intention'? Remember those unintended consequences or secondary gains? They could be sabotaging your success.

If you set a goal and you don't achieve it, chances are it's not important enough to you.

That may sound harsh and yet it's probably true. *If something is really important to you, what would you be willing to do or willing to sacrifice to achieve it?*

Let's take those big-ticket items first: stopping smoking, losing weight, and getting fit. I think it's true to say that we all know these are things we should do. If it's so obvious, why is it so hard to change? Even if you regularly engage in a behaviour that you hate, wish you could change, and think has no positive use whatsoever, then you are wrong. On some level, there is a positive intention. Identify the secondary gain. This is a big step towards changing the pattern, because, if you know what the intention is, you can very likely get the same outcome from a different behaviour.

If you are always running late, maybe there is a secondary gain from the excitement and drama it causes.

If you smoke or drink or eat chocolate when you are stressed, maybe it's because it helps you feel calm.

Once you have identified the positive intention, you can look for a healthier way to achieve the same result.

How else could you have some excitement in your life without making yourself late? Maybe sign up to do a parachute jump or embark on a new career or hobby.

How else could you feel calm when you are stressed? Maybe have a cup of tea, have a long bath, or phone a friend for a chat.

The next thing to think about is what you want. The difference between a dream and a goal is often just a plan. Simply writing down your goal and thinking about exactly what it is you want will dramatically increase your odds of achieving it.

Think beyond the goal

How will it feel when you have achieved your goal? Then what?

I know from personal experience how quickly that dopamine high can fade and how easy it is to return to old patterns. The minute I crossed the finish line at the London Marathon and had that medal placed over my head I felt awesome. I had done it. I had achieved my goal. Great, now I could stop. And I did. I stopped. No more training, no more healthy eating, no more heading towards something. And you guessed it, the weight went back on, and my fitness levels declined. I was literally dining out on the fact that I had done it.

One of the biggest challenges with my weight is that it is harder to be motivated to achieve a goal that you have already achieved once. That's why even gold medal Olympians are always striving for a new personal best. The goal of getting an Olympic gold isn't as motivating when you already have one. You have to find the new aspect that will re-ignite the fire.

Stop putting yourself on hold

You need patience for some dreams, yet make sure you do not put barriers in your own way.

Be careful of delaying your dreams and happiness.

Remember that bucket lists and goals are for events and not states.

Happiness is a state, and you can decide to be happy now.

If you find yourself saying things like, 'I'll be happy when... I get a new job, I'm earning more money, I'm more successful, I'm married, I'm thinner...' you are handing your happiness over to factors that are not entirely in your control.

How can you get it now, even just a little bit?

My dream was to live by the sea. For all the years in which that was not possible, you can bet that I had as many weekends and short trips by the sea as I could get away with.

Think about the goals you are working on. Would you call them goals or are they ideas or dreams?

> **"Remember, the single most important thing you can do to achieve a goal is to create one in the first place"**

Remember the commander and the platoon? Your conscious and unconscious mind? The commander needs to give really clear directions to the platoon, or they will find a way to cheat. The commander might say, 'We're doing this tomorrow' (or next week or next year). The platoon, our unconscious mind, is tricky. It knows that tomorrow never comes, and neither does next week or next year. Every day you will wake up with your platoon saying, 'It's okay, we're going to do that tomorrow.' You need to give yourself goals with no wriggle room. What date and even what time do you want to achieve this? Narrow it down to a date on the calendar.

The same applies to the goal itself. If the commander says you want to make 'more' money or achieve a 'faster' time, again, you have made it easy for your platoon to take the easiest option. Making one penny more is still more. Taking half a second off your time is faster, and yet that might not be what you had in mind.

The more specific you are about what you want to achieve, the more detailed the instructions will be to the platoon, so they have no choice but to achieve it. Think of it like sending a young child to do your shopping. How specific would you have to be to have a chance of getting what you wanted?

Once you have your goal clear in your mind, wake up every day with the intention of behaving as if it is guaranteed to happen. This will have the effect of activating a part of your brain that notices the things you are interested in. The platoon will keep a special eye out for anything that will help you achieve your goal. Have you ever decided to buy a specific make of car and suddenly you notice them all the time on the road? Have you started to work for a new company and suddenly you notice their TV ads when they previously passed you by? Have you decided to get fit and every radio ad, billboard and social media feed are only advertising gyms, trainers, and fitness classes?

It's called your Reticular Activation System. If your brain made you notice every piece of information that was available to you every day, you would go a bit crazy trying to keep up, so it filters out all the things it thinks you are not interested in, and it points out the things it thinks you will want to notice. When what matters to you changes, it's like asking the platoon to be on high alert for anything they think will be useful to you now.

It is very powerful to set out your goal as though it has already happened. It will trick your unconscious mind into thinking that you have already achieved it, so success is a foregone conclusion.

Let's time travel into the future and look back to now.

Close your eyes and bring to mind an image of you achieving your goal. It helps to see the image through your own eyes, so you do not see yourself in the picture. (When you see the image through your own eyes, this is called associated)

What can you see?

What can you hear?

How does it feel?

What are other people saying?

What have you learned on your journey?

Make the image as compelling as possible, then step out of the picture so you can see yourself achieving your goal as if you were an observer. (When you can see yourself in the image, this is called dissociated)

Capture your answers.

Today is _____
(Date - include day, month and year)

and I have_____
(What you have achieved?)

I feel _____
(How you are feeling now you achieved this?)

I learned _____
(What have you learned along the way?)

Now you have made your goal crystal clear, turn your attention to your breathing. Just notice your breath as you breathe in and out.

Imagine you're standing in an elevator. You're on the tenth floor. The elevator starts to travel downwards. As you watch the floor numbers descend... ten... nine... eight... seven... you notice you're starting to feel more relaxed. Six... five... halfway there now, feeling more focused and calm.

Four... three... two... one. You reach the bottom level, and the doors open onto the most stunning view. You see a passageway leading out into a beautiful, relaxing place. Notice the way the light and the colours draw you in as you walk through and into that beautiful natural environment. Here you can start to understand and see things in a new light.

It is like a sanctuary, your thinking place. Today we are going to wander to where we see a signpost that points in a number of different directions and one of these signpost directions points to your goals.

Follow its direction until you reach a place you feel is clearly designed for you to create and envision effective and powerful goals. It may be a special open space, or it may be a room in a house with an amazing view or somewhere else... just know this place has all the creative tools you need. Remember, inside your head you have an unlimited budget so it can be however you want it to be.

There you are in this special place – you notice there's exactly what you need to create a vision board. On this vision board you can write, paint, or draw your goals: it's a blank canvas for you to project your ideas onto.

See this really well-defined goal; see it actually happening. As you look at it, start to talk yourself through it using the present tense. As you look at it, describe what you see.

Notice how this looks. Really get a clear image of it. The final and really important trick is to step inside that vision board now... experience it first-hand as if you were really there doing it. Look through your own eyes.

Feel what it feels like. Experience your future goal as a current reality.

Finally, add some sparkle! Make it bright and shiny and shimmering.

Now have the you of the future say something back to the you of now, something really important and significant. Listen to what they say – right now.

Often, what that future you will say to the now you is, 'You can do this,' or, 'You deserve this,' or, 'It's going to be much easier than you could ever have imagined.' It may say something different, some piece of learning that it wants you to know.

Having visited this place for the first time, leave this special zone where you create goals. Now, wander out through the sanctuary and back into the elevator feeling relaxed. As you travel back from floor one to floor ten, you feel refreshed with a clear sense of exactly what it is that you are heading for right now.

You can visit this place as often as you want to, to get in touch with this goal or to build new ones.

10

HAVE YOU GOT CRABS?
YOU CHOOSE TO BELIEVE IF IT'S GOING TO BE, IT'S GOING TO BE ME

Once upon a time, there was a curious crab called Crab.

Crab lived in a rusty, old, blue bucket by the sea.

Crab didn't like the bucket very much; it wasn't just old, it was smelly, dirty, and very overcrowded.

That said, Crab had lived in the bucket all her life and didn't know if there was anything on the other side of the bucket, but she was curious. Crab spent her days squashed inside the bucket, daydreaming about whether other buckets even existed or if this was the only one in the whole world. She imagined there were but never really knew. The bucket felt familiar and warm, and even though there were many other crabs in there, they were her friends. They were everything she'd ever known.

One day, the curious crab decided she wanted to find out what was on the other side of the high, blue metal wall. She'd dreamed about this moment her whole life. She set herself a goal to climb the bucket wall in the next five minutes.

The grand climb began. Using all her grittitude, Crab began her ascent. When the other crabs noticed this great escape happening in front of them, they immediately started to pull her back down. Every time she attempted to scale the big blue wall, more and more of the crabs joined in and pulled her back into the bucket.

Crab went back to her place in the bucket and back to her daydreams.

'It was a silly idea. I fit in much better here anyway. It's warm and comfortable and these are my friends,' she thought to herself.

Have you got crabs in your life? A crab's mentality is much like our own human response to others embarking on self-improvement. So often, when people see others advancing, they subconsciously or consciously reach out to hold them back, with negative talk, gossip and attempts to persuade them it's better to stay in their bucket.

 "If you're around people holding you back... you've definitely got crabs!"

You will notice that people who display crab mentality show behaviours of jealousy, envy, and fear. *Fear of what?* I hear you ask. They may feel threatened, they may fear others becoming more successful than them, or they may feel rejected or abandoned by you.

A crab leaving the bucket forces all the other crabs to ask themselves uncomfortable questions. It triggers the voices in their own heads about what they have achieved in their lives, families or careers. It challenges us to the core when someone 'like us' does something 'people like us don't do'. You're changing the rules of what 'people like us' do so instead of wondering what is possible they decide you're strange, you're weird, you're not normal, you don't fit in.

This crab mindset is worsened when it spreads through a group of people. The result is bullying, bitterness and betrayal between peers. They will gang up together to prevent someone getting ahead.

The crab mentality is not just about preventing people from making progress physically – it involves targeting them mentally too.

People with this mentality will often try to weaken the morale of others, attacking their self-confidence and making them believe they're not good enough to 'escape'.

How do you know you're a Crab?

A crab doesn't normally know they are a crab. These are their characteristics:

A crab loves to say, 'You've changed.' (And not in a positive way!)

A crab doesn't encourage their friends and family to pursue their dreams.

A crab has sharp words.

Imagine you're going for a promotion at work which will make you the manager of the team you have been part of for a number of years. Whilst you are clearly the best person for the job, the people you work with start to change their behaviour towards you. I see this a lot in my corporate work.

You were their friend, part of the team. Now you're 'the boss'.

Instead of your friends and teammates supporting you and helping you in your new role, they take advantage, stop including you in social interactions, and complain behind your back that you're behaving differently.

In sport, moving from amateur to professional, the teammates you met during your earlier learning years now feel left behind as you elevate through the ranks to the next level.

At school, the clever kid, instead of feeling proud of their achievements, is made to feel like an outsider, called a try-hard or a sweat for wanting to do more, be more.

In life, we all get put into a bucket in one way or another.

We all share similar social groups or 'buckets' through relationships such as being classmates, co-workers, family members, or being in the same friendship group.

When people deem you to be in the same bucket as them, they might try to pull you down when they notice that you're growing and climbing out of the bucket.

People usually don't care about those they deem to be less successful than them, or way more successful than them. These situations are both outside of the only bucket they've ever known. Yet when you're at that peer level, people start comparing themselves to you and seeing you as competition.

> "Everyone loves you until you become the competition"

That's why strangers might be more supportive of your goals, dreams, and success than friends and family. Many people want you to do well.

And in the real world, the crabs in the bucket situation similarly backfires. Why? Because in human relationships, having mutual enemies does not make you friends. The oppression strategy of the collective is no basis for bonding. Rather, it creates an atmosphere of suspicion and distrust – you have to constantly watch your back before they come for you next.

Despite these adverse consequences, you still find people who seem to be convinced that the only way to succeed is to bring others down.

Another example of crab mentality is when friends fail to support each other, even when it would literally cost them *nothing*. For example, a person invites a friend to like their new business page on Facebook, yet the friend withholds the like, perhaps due to a tinge of jealousy.

Sometimes people withhold complimenting their peers who do well because it makes them feel inferior. Or they attribute this person's success to chance, making excuses such as, 'They were lucky,' rather than recognising their hard work.

Some individuals might refuse to recommend a peer for a role they know they would excel at – because they are worried that the person will become more successful than them. They might also not pass on a useful contact or opportunity to a peer who requires assistance to reach a goal.

Another way that a crab mentality manifests is when people mock their friends for their goals and aspirations. Out of jealousy and their own insecurity, they might try to convince the person that what they're working towards is impossible. The basis of their remark is usually the fact that they've never done it, or *they've never seen anyone else do it*. This is never a valid argument.

They may even do it out of love, thinking that holding you back is protecting you from failure, protecting you from pain, keeping you safe, keeping you close.

Who's in your bucket?

If you are experiencing any of these traits, it's time to find a new bucket.

As you achieve personal growth it may mean having to break ties with the people in your bucket and find a new peer group of people who share your new values, achievements and aspirations.

The more successful you are, the more times you will go through this process of moving on and leaving others behind.

This is often how we discover our true friends and supporters who stay with us as we climb higher.

You can, of course, go back and visit old buckets from time to time. It can be exciting and useful to see how far you've come. Not everyone will be happy to see you and have you remind them of all they haven't done and the opportunities they didn't get or didn't take.

Protect your own boundaries. You may have had some luck along the way and yet you should be proud of what you have achieved. If your old 'friends' start saying 'crabby' things, maybe they were just crabs all along.

Kay's Story - Losing Shaun

When I was fourteen years old, my cousin took his own life. Being in the room when this news was shared with my auntie and uncle changed my life. I didn't know then just how much of an impact it would have.

The things I saw and felt that day will stay with me forever. I've managed to reframe the memory to the point that I'm no longer affected by it day to day. But it did change me in a massive way. I was always older than my years even then, but I grew up so much more in that one moment. And as much as the confusion, despair and grief took hold of me, I also had the overwhelming feeling that I had to get out if I wanted something better than his fate had been. I had to make it happen.

I decided to become a solicitor. Word had it that they got paid well and it could be my ticket out of town, so I set out on my mission. I enrolled in Latin as one of my options in high school. I put together a letter listing some of my skills and what I felt I could bring to the role of an assistant Saturday girl.

I spent weekend mornings visiting every solicitor practice in the small town where I lived, letter in hand, and made the offer of bottomless cups of tea and coffee in return for observing the solicitors at work. Time had become very precious all of a sudden. I had none to waste. My obsession with being successful had become my only focus and in many ways a lifeline.

Whilst people smiled and thanked me, I didn't hear from any of them. I went back in one at a time to be told that if there was any news they would get in touch. They never did.

A year later, our already volatile family situation became even worse. My world collapsed again. At sixteen I decided it was time to go, and it had to be now. I had left school and started my college course studying Law. It was the hardest decision of my life to leave my family home. By far the hardest part was leaving my younger siblings behind. I believed if I could make myself stronger, I would be able to help them get stronger too.

I left. I got away.

I spent my days at college studying Law, evenings at school studying criminology and juggling three part-time jobs to fund everything. Thank goodness for the kindness of a friend whom I had met on my course, and her family, who let me live with them rent-free for a while.

Despite all of this, I still didn't feel much happier than I had at home, and two years later I returned.

My parents' relationship continued to deteriorate and eventually broke down completely. A choking, sick feeling started screaming at me again – I had to leave that place.

By then I had met my boyfriend (now husband) and we had our daughter. Together we moved away. For a week before I moved, I cried every day. Like ending a long-term relationship, I knew we were over forever. I knew this time that I wouldn't come back.

My obsession with work got stronger until it became unhealthy. It wasn't until I learned to stop, reflect and be patient that everything really came together. The combination of practice, patience, persistence, and passion took time and effort. It was super uncomfortable to stop running from the problems and face them head-on.

I became financially secure, and able to truly live my life purpose every day through my work, helping people face their own cold, hard truths and fulfil their life purpose. A few years (and tears) later I started my business, which grew to be very successful.

The biggest learnings?

Moving away gave me the space I needed to discover and build my grit, face who I was, make friends with myself and rid myself of the guilt I felt for all the shitty things that had happened in the past.

Running away to another place doesn't make you happy; it's just geography. You have to choose to be happy, to be grateful, to learn to love every detail of the mess, the struggle and the heartache as the most vulnerable you.

Once you have learnt to accept that there is no good or bad, right or wrong, happy or sad, you can just be you. No matter where you are.

It may not be easy, but it will be worth it.

Are you happy in the bucket you are in?

What will you lose if you stay where you are?

What will you gain if you stay where are?

What will you gain if you choose to change?

What could you lose if you choose to change?

Who are your crabs?

Who doesn't want you to succeed?

Who constantly puts you down?

Who doesn't support you?

How will your success impact your family and friends?

What is more important to you: achieving your dreams or meeting other people's expectations?

Who can you rely on for unconditional support?

How can you create your own support network?

11

CAGOULES, SUNSCREEN, AND BOBBLE HATS
YOU CHOOSE TO BELIEVE STATE IS EVERYTHING

Throughout our lives we are offered advice, feedback and opinions from everywhere. Some of it is helpful and some is complete and utter shite. It's not always easy to work out which advice to listen to and which to ignore. When you choose to believe that all behaviour has a positive intention it makes it much easier to also choose whether to accept or decline the feedback. That too is your choice.

 "Never accept feedback from someone from whom you wouldn't ask advice"

As coaches, the primary reason people come to us is to better handle what their life, work or sport is throwing at them. Our role is not to do anything for them. I appreciate this may sound odd.

You can't fix something that is not broken, and you are not broken. You may feel lost, confused or uncertain at a crossroads in your life but that doesn't make you broken. *If we do everything for you, how will you handle things when we are not there?*

Our part is to add more helpful resources to your backpack and remove the old ones that no longer serve you, so you can choose your own life story. And whilst travelling with others is fun, you know you can handle the parts where you are doing it alone.

It's a bit like you are standing behind a massive brick wall wondering if there is anything on the other side. Once you know there is, all you need are the tools to get over, under or around that brick wall to reach the other side.

In the movie *Wild*, starring Reese Witherspoon, Cheryl Strayed treks the Pacific Coast Trail as a way to cope with her grief. She nicknames her backpack 'Monster' as it weighs over seventy pounds. In a scene where a more experienced hiker takes her overflowing backpack and empties out the entire contents, she has a stark realisation that she has been carrying the weight of the world on her shoulders the entire time. Cheryl packed for everything, and at various parts of her adventure the things were useful to her, yet when they were no longer useful, she forgot to leave them behind.

She reassesses every item, carefully considering if that resource would be helpful in the rest of her adventure. She whittles it down by questioning the need to carry the weight of each item, followed by the decision to throw away every single item that is not essential.

She even leaves the pages of the map that she has already covered and are now behind her.

We can all be a bit like that.

We can all take on the weight of the world, the stresses and strains of other people's stories, and spend years holding onto 'why me', 'I don't understand', and 'what if'.

No matter what you do or what someone else does, as far as the behaviour is concerned, everyone is always doing the best they can with the resources they have available to them. Sometimes they have packed their cagoule, and sometimes they've packed their cagoule, sunscreen, bobble hat and the kitchen sink.

Grittitude is about doing the best you can with what you have. It's not about being perfect, it's about learning and growing and making progress one step at a time, and knowing you have everything you need right now to take that next step.

You could make do with a limited kit and try and make it work for you. And you don't need to wait till you have every resource available at your fingertips. When you are feeling relaxed and calm and at your best, you will naturally feel more resourceful. When you are stressed and tired you will feel unresourceful.

CAGOULES, SUNSCREEN, AND BOBBLE HATS

It's about being in the right state, not a right state!

Behaviour is dependent on your state. I bet you behave in a totally different way when you feel positive and motivated than when you feel miserable and frustrated. *Is it the chicken or the egg? Did the bad state change your behaviour or did the behaviour change your state?*

It always starts with your state.

The results we get depend upon our behaviours and our behaviours depend on our 'state' (what's going on in our minds and our physiology). So, once you recognise that you are in charge of your own mind and you can control and choose the state you are in, you can also choose the behaviours and results.

Your physiology has a massive impact on your state. It is totally impossible to 'run' bad mood state in your neurology while doing good mood state physiology. *Have you ever been in a bad mood when you are dancing?* (Unless you were being forced to dance!) Of course not!

If you are in an unresourceful state – negative, bored, fed up, frustrated, cross, angry, etc. – recognise that you are in control of it and change it. But how do you 'change it'? One of the quickest ways is to change your physiology. Stand up, tense your muscles, smile and say, inside your head, 'Yes, yes, yes, yes, yes,' in an excited voice. Your bad mood will be eliminated.

There is no need to be in an unresourceful state unless you choose to be. This officially means you can never really 'enjoy' feeling miserable again as deep down you will know that you are choosing to do it and you could just as easily change it.

How else can you change your state? I bet you have a song, or many songs, that instantly put you in a good mood. You probably also have songs that make you cry. Create a playlist for your mood. When you need to change your state, hit play.

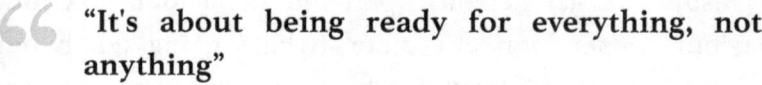

> "It's about being ready for everything, not anything"

If you want to be ready for any eventuality, you'll find yourself packing for every kind of weather. Have you found yourself packing your sunscreen and your cagoule just in case? This is the joy of the British weather.

When you know you can choose your state, you can feel assured that whatever happens, even things you could not possibly have predicted, you will be able to adapt and cope.

Alex's Story

Alex was in love. She had met Chris, and after just a few wonderful weeks, she was already making plans for a lifetime together. Of course, there was bickering about who should pay for dinner, how many times a week they saw their friends and what movie to watch, but none of that really mattered. She was happy and radiant. One evening, after a night at the cinema, Chris looked concerned. She asked what was on his mind and he said, 'I don't love you any more. I can't do this,' and walked away.

The following day, Alex called in sick to work. She didn't have the energy to get out of bed. She felt too sad. Over the next few days, she stayed in bed, only venturing as far as the sofa, bathroom, and back to bed again, feeling lost, confused, and angry.

When I asked her to come out for dinner or if I could come and see her, she would refuse, preferring to stay in the comfort of her home with her thoughts and sadness. I went to see her in an attempt to talk her around and persuade her to come for a walk. I struggled to hide my shock at the state of the place and the state of her! She had been eating rubbish food, confirmed by the pile of takeout boxes by the bin and the overflowing dirty dishes in the sink, she still hadn't got herself dressed and had clearly stopped showering and washing her hair. The house was a mess. She was a mess.

She hadn't heard anything from Chris for over two weeks. Then, out of the blue, she got a message.

'Hey, I know you probably don't want to speak to me, but I have to explain. I'm so sorry for leaving. I've made a massive mistake. Can we talk?'

Despite two weeks of deep depression, these four sentences and three seconds had a transformational effect. As if a bolt of electricity had surged through her body, she came back to life.

Despite my thoughts, judgements, and anger (*seriously! I've been here for you, and this asshole sends you one message and you're happy again?*), and despite the anguish she had put herself through over those last two weeks, in that moment, there was no mistaking that she was back.

Before even replying to the message, she jumped off the sofa and looked around the room as though seeing the mess for the first time, then looked down at the tea-stained jumper, saggy joggers, and mismatching socks she had clearly worn well past the appropriate date with the washing machine.

Within a few hours the house was tidied, cleaned and Alex was showered, made up and ready to face the world again. More specifically, Chris.

Chris didn't create the state Alex got herself into. The meaning Alex placed on Chris's words and actions created the state.

We can all recall moments which have the power to change how we feel—past events, moments, and experiences.

I wonder if you could remember one of those experiences right now, and recall the feeling, right now.

I want you to get yourself into a bad mood. I promise we will only do this for a few short moments.

I'm curious…

How did you do that? What did you have to think about to make yourself be in a bad mood?

Think about your body language first. Maybe you needed to slump down in the chair, hunch your shoulders, and turn down the corners of your mouth. Perhaps you needed to think of a time when you had some news that made you feel bad.

What do you need to say to yourself to make your mood even worse?

Is it a movie playing in your mind?

Okay, that's enough. Shake it off now, change your posture, make yourself smile and see how quickly that bad mood can vanish. I personally enjoy a few moments of Taylor Swift's *Shake It Off*, and if I really need to add a bolt of electricity, I'm partial to a bit of Katrina and the Waves' *Walking on Sunshine*. You choose what helps you shake it off.

Now let's experiment with what will put you into a great mood.

How will you sit? Will you stand up? Or better still, will you dance? Turn the corners of your mouth up and remember a time when you felt totally happy and amazing.

What words are you saying to yourself that easily make you feel great?

> **You have the power to change your mood whenever you want to. You have the choice; you hold the key. You can create your own story.**

In my many conversations with Alex over the two weeks of misery, she would often say, 'I'm not surprised he left: I'm not pretty enough; I'm not interesting enough; he must have found someone better.' Alex spoke to herself in such painful ways, and often enough that she started to believe they were true.

Think about the things you say to yourself every day.

Are they helpful or hurtful?

If you tell yourself, 'I'm no good,' often enough, you will start to believe it.

By the way, Alex and Chris are no longer together. Their relationship ended in the realisation that they weren't right for each other.

Adi's Story

Adi was still a teenager when he left his sports team.

He said, 'I'm not sure what's wrong with me. I don't feel well, I'm always tired and I have no motivation to do anything. I just don't feel like myself.'

I asked him, 'Tell me who you *do* feel like? What's his name? Describe him to me.'

He answered easily. 'He's lazy; he has long hair and spends all day playing on his computer; he wants to eat pizza and stay in bed all day. If he had a name, it would be Jed.'

He was visibly surprised that he was able to answer me so easily. He found it strange that somehow his brain had easily offered this information.

Then I asked Adi to tell me about who he is when he is at his best.

Adi said, 'He's so cool – he's the man! He is so confident, he walks with his chest high and he loves the spotlight. If he had a name, it would be Lionel.'

We discussed how these people are parts of him. They are simply different states that show up for a reason, so we explored more.

I said, 'What do you get from being in a 'Jed' state of mind?'

He sat in silence for a few moments, pondering the question. Then he responded with, 'I get to stop. My life is so busy and there's so much to do. It feels like I'm doing it for everyone else. Jed lets me get away from it all. It's just that he's turning up a bit too much lately and it's affecting me and my performance.

Then I asked Adi to tell me about Lionel and what he gets from being in a 'Lionel' state of mind?

He said, 'I love it when he's around. I feel amazing, on top of the world, in fact. I couldn't have him around all the time as it would be intense, but I really enjoy it when he's there.'

I asked, 'How do we work out an agreement between you, Jed and Lionel so that you can still be Jed sometimes but not all the time, and Lionel when you decide you want him around?'

We talked through when it was appropriate to do the Jed behaviours and when it was appropriate to do the Lionel behaviours and how we could notice when each showed up.

By giving each an identity it stopped Adi from feeling out of control and put him firmly in control. He was now able to make those behaviours a choice.

When we reconnected just a week later, the Xbox had been put away and Adi had got back into the gym. He even looked different – lighter, happy. Two weeks after that, he secured a new contract with a new sports team.

Think about a recent example where you had an unwanted outcome. Maybe you got angry, upset or jealous?

Take some time to consider these questions. You might want to write down your answers.

What triggered your response?

What was the 'story' you told yourself?

What was your resulting state?

What was your reaction or response?

What did you say and do? What words did you use, and what body language?

What was the outcome for you and/or others?

How did it impact the rest of your day?

How did it impact the people around you?

What could you do differently?

How could you change the story you told yourself?

Every failure is one step closer to success. You will embarrass yourself, you will fail.

Bounce Forward

I choose not to believe in bouncing back. I don't want to go back.

Bounce Forward

12

TWENTY SECONDS
YOU CHOOSE TO BELIEVE IN THE COURAGE TO FAIL

Kay's Story - Learning To Swim

I knew people were looking at me when I walked in, judging me. I couldn't help but make full eye contact in a *'yes, I know you're looking at me, knobhead'* kind of way.

People staring at others who don't look like them or who do things that sit outside of the norm still triggered me. Judgemental behaviour triggered me. I worry about what someone else might do in that situation, someone younger, less confident, less able to handle it than I could.

On this particular day I was at the local swimming pool. I had arrived at the pool complete with speedo costume and goggles, excited, nervous and ready to go.

Sitting on the cold, white plastic chair, I heard parents whispering to their children to stop staring at the lady. The lady was me; I was the lady.

I was thirty-three years old, not the typical age for a first swimming lesson.

A little girl of four or five years old said goodbye to the instructor and climbed out of the pool. She ran to her mum, who praised her for how well she had done in her lesson.

The swim instructor shouted my name. I was up next.

I still felt the fear bubbling up inside as I walked towards the pool ladder, regressing further into nine-year-old me with each step. I was as terrified in that moment as the day it happened.

If the last twenty-four years had taught me anything, it was that there's nothing more paralysing than the feeling of helplessness that comes with this fear. And if I was going to keep breaking through other barriers in my life, this pattern of fear-filled behaviour had to be broken through too.

Today was the day all that bubbling fear would be gone.

Twenty-four years earlier

I went on a weekend trip to Pontins with the Morris dancing team. All my mates and no parents! What an adventure. We sang and danced all the way there as we got high on sugary sweets on our incredible double-decker bus which took us to all our competitions.

Still experiencing a sugar rush, we almost toppled on top of each other with giddy excitement as we piled off the bus. We had some free time before evening dance practice, and the girls decided it would be a good idea to go swimming. It was one of those fancy pools with a wave machine.

Whilst the other girls got excited, I was feeling nervous. That's not true; I was absolutely papping my pants! They say that after every high comes a low and mine was epic. The very thought of getting in the water, especially unsupervised, terrified me, let alone one with a wave machine. I'd seen these wave machines in action before at the local pool and they should have called them tsunami tanks.

We pushed each other toward our Morris dancing coach, saying, 'You ask... no you... she likes you.' To cut a medium story short I ended up in front of our coach looking up like Oliver Twist about to ask for more. Not only did I not want to ask, I didn't want her to say yes. I did not want to go!

Surely, she'd say no. I mean, who would let a bunch of eight to eleven-year-old kids go swimming in a tsunami tank alone?

If I refused, I feared the girls would ask a zillion questions about why and taunt me. Maybe they would even fall out with me, completely reject me from the group and that would ruin the whole weekend. I'd be on my own in my room on what was supposed to be the best weekend ever. That's the story my quite annoying brain managed to create for me.

The next few minutes have been completely deleted from my mind, like a silent movie playing in slow motion. The sound came back on full as I heard the word *yes*. What? She said yes. Shit! She said yes! How the hell did that happen?

I felt the blood running away from my head, draining down my body and into my toes. My insides got colder as I started shutting down. The inevitable was drawing closer and I'd made it happen. Feeling dizzy I steadied myself, whilst doing my best to plaster a big 'I'm happy' smile on my face.

Even then I couldn't help but notice how we were all experiencing the same thing in a different way. Everyone looked so excited. You know the feeling, right? When you're feeling anxious, with low mood and low confidence and everyone else seems to be fine, yet you get that sinking feeling in the pit of your stomach? You're the only one that feels this way. Everyone else is 'loving life' except you.

Well, it was just like that, and I couldn't understand why I was so freaking scared.

I felt so embarrassed. The voice in my head reminded me that the others could all swim, that I was a rubbish swimmer. It proceeded to deliver paralysing post it notes to my mind, pointing out all the times in the past that I'd been laughed at in swimming lessons when I'd sat on the side, and the occasion when I failed to get the stupid rubber brick from the bottom of the pool. They flashed up like a rapid slide show in full colour.

The horn sounded. My body stiffened, frozen as the ripples from the wave machine started to pulsate in the water.

I allowed the rhythm of the ripples to fall in time with the motion of my body. I was gently holding on to the side of the pool, feeling almost relaxed. This wasn't as bad as I had expected it to be. Then, with what seemed like no warning at all, the small ripples started to get bigger and bigger, splashing into my face. They were massive now and the waves kicked in full force, crashing fiercely over the sides of the pool. The chlorinated water shot up my nose, burning it from the inside as it travelled into and down my throat. I removed one hand from the side of the pool to hold my nose and before I knew what was happening, I was swept into the middle of the pool. I couldn't reach the bottom anymore and the tsunami was in full motion. I felt like a sock in a massive washing machine.

I vaguely remember everything going silent and the next thing I knew I was lying by the side of the pool with lots of people staring over me. The lifeguard had jumped in to save me.

I could not handle this – the embarrassment, the shame, and the fact that the whole wave machine had been stopped and I had ruined everyone's fun. I returned to the cabin alone, shaken, humiliated, and embarrassed. I never visited a pool or spoke about it ever again.

As I lowered myself into the pool twenty-four years later, the smell of chlorine wafted up my nose and everything came flooding back.

I tentatively set off, my mind full of images of that moment, my heart pounding in the same way it had then. I'd done my research. This pool was twenty foot long, shallower than my height and no tsunami tank! I can't have moved more than five metres when I started to cough and splutter. It was like I was a nine-year-old again. I reset and went again, this time with the voice of my instructor in my mind sharing gentle encouragement, advice, and recognition. We laughed; we joked.

She said three things:

- Breathing underwater is like meditation.
- You are strong and have great technique.
- Buy a nose clip!

You know what? I discovered I'm actually a decent swimmer: I always was.

What are you afraid of?

 "Laughter is poison to fear"

GEORGE R.R. MARTIN

When was the last time you laughed?

I mean properly laughed from the pit of your stomach all the way through your body, eye-watering cries of uncontrollable laughter.

When was the last time you felt fear?

Fear of failure, rejection, not being good enough. Fear of being left behind, left out or forgotten about, assuming you have got to be so much better than everyone else to succeed.

Whether it's an important work presentation, an exam or a sports event, do you perform well when practising and then become unbearably tense on the day of the big event?

If you experience feelings of anxiety and nervousness at the most inconvenient moments, you could just stop showing up at all. I wasn't very happy with my body shape as a kid so the idea of stripping off into a costume in front of all my school-mates was terrifying to me. Instead, I would pretend to forget my costume, fake an injury or illness, anything to get out of swimming lessons. I would sit on the side-lines watching friends have fun in the water and leave feeling guilty and left out. If you have ever felt this way about anything in your life, it may be helpful to learn what's taking over inside and some strategies to step into the feeling of discomfort until it becomes comfortable – without having to wait twenty-four years!

The coordination and movement required of your body to perform becomes very difficult when you are in a tense state. It can feel like a real battle, leaving you frustrated and confused. Tension happens as a result of the pressure and expectations you and possibly others around you, put on you.

The whole body is sent into high alert as your nervous system sends a signal to look out for potential threats. These are not real external threats, but threats to our deeper, hidden beliefs about identity and success.

The mind doesn't know the difference between real and self-made threats and therefore releases cortisol (the stress hormone) into your body to prepare it for survival, and you keep this state running through the negative narrative and images you create in your mind.

Sometimes you need some of this cortisol because your body is preparing for competition. However, at other times it can be unhealthy, unsustainable, and destructive, not only for your performance, but also for your health and wellbeing.

How does it show up for you?

Whilst it may feel challenging to be open to exploring what lurks under the surface of performance anxiety, it is also liberating, powerful and transformational if you choose to start by having the courage to see what is hiding in there.

Perhaps you worry about being judged on social media about your performance, or you become highly self-critical following a social event, work presentation or sports competition.

Perhaps you focus on being perfect in everything you do, which presents itself as an obsession to practise and practise until it's 100% right.

These feelings are driven by a fear of failure.

Fear is running in all of us all the time. The perception and grandeur of a specific event can really turn that volume up on fear. It can be hard to know it's there, as it presents itself in different ways in different people and environments.

All fear is counterproductive to the state you really want to create when you are in performance mode. It zaps all the enjoyment and excitement out of your experience. If I asked you to recall a time when you performed at your best, I doubt you'd tell me about the time you felt tense, stressed and nervous; you'd share with me the time you were having fun and relaxed. You'd tell me about a time when everything felt effortless and just flowed – a win from within that led to a public victory.

What can you do about it?

Let go of the fear

Whilst internal fear feels very real, it's important to be honest with yourself. Your fear is mostly self-made.

If you ignore the unhelpful story that is running your show (and therefore the feeling it is creating inside you), it will get louder and will keep coming back, triggering the release of too much cortisol which will drain your adrenal glands, leaving you fatigued and burnt out.

Accept that fear is real for all of us, including you, and bring it out into the light.

Get familiar with how fear looks, sounds and feels

It's time to get to know when and how fear shows up for you. Remember, it is just an energy that needs space to pass through us, yet we often try to suppress it. We just need to know when fear has arrived and how it shows up for us personally, so we can see it and allow it through. Next time you feel it ask yourself these questions:

Where do you feel it in your body?

Does it move?

If it has a colour, what colour does it have?

Does it have a temperature?

What texture is it?

Is there an image you associate with fear?

Creating it as an entity like this enables you to separate it from yourself and the hidden depth of your mind, allowing you to be more objective about what triggers your internal fear and how it impacts your performance. You can begin to look at this fear and notice how your behaviour, mood and energy change when it shows up.

Who do you become when fear is hanging out with you?

The more you practise fear management, the less power fear has to take hold of you, especially when you want to be at your best. You create the mental space to choose your response to fear.

Fear can't survive when it is brought out into the light – it becomes powerless.

You might not need to be brave for long

I was watching the movie *We Bought a Zoo* based on the true story of Benjamin Mee, and I came across this wonderful quote:

'You know, sometimes all you need is twenty seconds of insane courage. Just literally twenty seconds of just embarrassing bravery. And I promise you, something great will come of it.' *Benjamin Mee.*

I love this! Take a moment to think about it. *How long do you need to be brave for?* He's right, often twenty seconds is all you need, maybe even less. I only needed to have courage for a second or two to get into the pool. It only takes a few seconds to pick up the phone and make the call you are putting off or to walk into the room.

It also reminds us not to rehearse the fear. There is no point in allowing yourself to get into the state of fear and readiness when you lie in bed the night before. Right now, you are lying in your bed, and you are safe. The time to let yourself get into the state is just twenty seconds before.

Warren's Story

Warren had worked in the same company for twelve years. When he joined, he only planned for it to be for a short while but then he had a manager, Shane, who inspired and motivated him to turn it into a career.

As time went on, he continued to be supported and inspired by Shane. As Shane progressed into more senior roles, Warren rose through the ranks too.

Then Shane left.

Now Warren feels abandoned by Shane and overlooked by his new boss.

He said, 'I feel like I have to start all over again building a relationship with my new manager. He has no idea about my experience or skills, and every time opportunities come up, he doesn't even consider me.'

I asked him what he could do to help his new manager understand what skills he had and what motivated and inspired him. He thought for a moment, then realised that he had become so used to having a manager who already knew all about him, it hadn't occurred to him that it was up to him to ask for what he wanted.

We discussed what he could do to prepare for a meeting with his new manager. He recognised that he needed to reflect on all that he had achieved over the twelve years and what he wanted his future to look like. It was then his responsibility to have a conversation about how best to manage and motivate him.

I asked him when he thought he could set up the meeting with his boss.

He said, 'Well, maybe in a few weeks as right now isn't the best time. There is a lot of change going on in the business.'

This made me question how important this really was to him and whether the change was just an excuse. He admitted that he was reluctant to have the conversation as he didn't want to make the relationship worse. In fact, the change was creating new opportunities that he thought he was missing out on because his boss wasn't including him in discussions.

We talked about the impact on his career of not having the courage to have a short conversation. I challenged him to consider what the worst outcome could be from talking to his manager about what he wanted. At this point, he realised that there really wasn't any risk in picking up the phone and asking to talk about his future.

Six weeks later, we met again and I asked how his relationship with his manager was now.

He said, 'Oh that, that sorted itself out. I called him about the changes, and he asked me if I wanted to move into a new department. I started my new role last week!'

It's funny how once a problem is resolved you look back and it doesn't even look like it ever was a problem. After all, it couldn't have been that big a deal if it got resolved so quickly.

I reminded him that it hadn't 'sorted itself out'. He had sorted it out himself by taking action.

Mandy's Story

Mandy is a powerlifter and a phenomenal athlete. She has been competing in her sport professionally for many years. Then, in what seemed to her to be overnight, she developed a performance-crippling fear of lifting. Every time she even thought about approaching the platform to lift, the fear engulfed her entire body. It had got to the point that she started to pull out of national and international competitions. She made up excuses like being injured or unwell because she couldn't face telling people that she was a powerlifter with a fear of lifting.

I could see from her body language that even though we were sitting comfortably in the safety of her home, she had mentally gone to the platform, so I asked, 'What do you like to do when you're not lifting?'

Mandy glanced over at the dining room table where a half-completed jigsaw lay and replied, 'I love jigsaws. Hours can go by without me looking up from a good jigsaw!'

'I see this one looks like a *Star Wars* theme,' I said. She replied with some excitement at my interest, 'Yes, I must admit I'm also a sci-fi geek. I can watch those films for days!'

After a few minutes of talking about things she loved to do, her state was completely different. She was relaxed and calm.

I said, 'If you were doing a jigsaw right now, and the next piece you added revealed you looking at the event that triggered your fear earlier, what would you see?'

There was an immediate burst of emotion, and tears rolled down her face. I encouraged her to let all those tears flow, as the image, whatever it was, had unlocked the door to the fear she had been subconsciously holding onto.

I asked her to close her eyes and keep adding pieces to that jigsaw in her mind. After a few moments, her sounds of pain and upset turned to laughter, uncontrollable roars of laughter, as those tears kept rolling.

I asked her to share with me what was happening now.

Mandy replied, 'I'm hanging from the claw of some weird robot thing hanging over a video clip of me doing a lift. I failed the squat and my spotter failed to catch the bar... but it looks super funny because I'm inside a cartoon sci-fi movie. It's really weird.'

I asked, 'Did this really happen?'

She said yes, but not exactly as she was seeing it. 'There was a time last year when my spotter failed to catch my bar when I failed a lift, but I'd completely forgotten about it.'

'There we go,' I said. 'We have unlocked the door, found the moment this fear was created, and now it's time to let it go.' I checked with Mandy whether it would be okay to let go of this emotion today.

Her reply came quickly: 'Hell, yes!'

I said, 'So now we are here and you can see it from a safe distance, what can you take as learnings from this moment in time?'

After a short pause Mandy replied with three things:

- I was okay.
- I didn't get hurt.
- It's only happened once in thousands of lifts.

I asked, 'Would it be okay to take those learnings now and let go of any old, unhelpful emotions now?'

Her body shifted further, her shoulders dropped away from her ears and her eyes shone brighter. And she replied that yes, it would.

After a few moments, Mandy took a few breaths and said, 'I feel so different. It's like a black cloud has been lifted and I get to lift this afternoon!' As soon as the words left her mouth, her hand flew up to cover it. 'I can't believe I just said that! But I really can't wait!'

Three hours later I received this message: 'I had ZERO fear. I didn't even get spotters for my top set! I let brave Mandy take over.'

> "How would your life change if you chose to be brave for just twenty seconds?"

These sound like really simple questions and yet the answers have the power to change your life.

What would you do if you were guaranteed to be successful?

What's the worst that can happen if you don't succeed first time?

What will you learn about yourself if you try?

13

SAY YES TO THE MESS

YOU CHOOSE TO BELIEVE THE MESS IS PART OF THE PROCESS

Kay's Story – The Clear-Out

I spent the whole day clearing the kitchen – it's one of those jobs that you wish you'd never started but once it's finished you're happy you did.

I love a good clear-out. I normally set off on my mission like a burst of sunshine, with real energy and excitement about how everything will look and how I will feel better once it's done. I can imagine the faces of my family returning home as they smile and make comments about how clean and tidy our home looks and smells.

I first make sure the house is empty of people, then I bang up the stereo and prepare to sing a few out-of-tune renditions of Tina Turner. The house being empty also makes the big reveal even more exciting. Work in secret and the *ta-dah* moment will be even greater!

I put on some of my favourite music and turn up the volume. That's my cue to start emptying the cupboards.

I make little piles of items:

- To keep
- To organise
- To store somewhere else
- To throw away

I particularly enjoy digging deep inside the dark depths of a space and finding things I thought I'd lost, items and memories that once played an important role discarded and forgotten beneath a pile of serviettes or at the back of a cupboard.

As the minutes turn into hours, and hours, and hours… I look around the room to find many large piles, most of which I don't even recall creating. They are all getting muddled up and falling into each other, and I can't even remember whether some are things to keep or throw away.

I plough on, one cupboard at a time, thinking to myself, 'This is going to be great.' I have little dividers for each area of the drawer or cupboard and labels to easily see where things are. It's going to save me so much time in the future and I'll feel so much more relaxed knowing everything's in its place.

The clock keeps ticking and time seems to disappear as I work.

As if by magic I am halted out of my deep focused flow by the feeling of hungry screaming from my stomach. It's at that moment I realise I haven't eaten. My body starts to feel heavy and my eyes wander around soaking up the complete and utter mess I have created!

Why did I ever think it was a good idea to even start? The beautiful picture I had in my mind has faded significantly, replaced with a large helping of self-doubt. Why did I even start, how did I really think I could do this alone, and where is everyone anyway? They never help! I am so annoyed at my husband for not helping. What was he thinking, leaving me to do this alone? I've completely underestimated the time I needed to do this!

The relatively neat piles are now scattered all over the place and making a right mess. People have started arriving home. It's much later than I realised. They walk in with no regard for the gallant effort I've made in organising our home. All they can see is mess and turmoil.

I could cry... shall I stop and cry or find a way to keep going? Maybe I'll do both.

What I do know is that I am well and truly sunk inside the messy bit in the middle.

How do you know you're in the middle, I hear you ask? ... Because it feels like an uncontrollable, unachievable, overwhelming mess.

None of us knows how our story ends, and often we can't know if we really are in the middle or not because we don't know for sure when the end is, but we can have a really good guess by checking in on how it feels. If it feels like one or all of these things, we're probably in the middle!

What do we do about it?

We navigate through and engage with this messy middle for what it is. It's another moment in time, but more than that, it is where the magic seems to happen. We all have something innately resilient within us that knows how to evolve, that has a determination even if it feels fragile, uncertain and doubtful. Even that version of you can find enough determination to keep hold of it; we can still creatively and wilfully enact meaningful change.

Personal growth is rough. If I told you it was going to be hard you may not have even started, yet if you find a path through development that is easy, it probably does not lead anywhere.

When we feel safe, we are generally at our best. We are vulnerable, open, playful, compassionate and loving.

 "Keep your mind strong and your body will follow"

Here's the thing…

Navigating your way through the messy bit in the middle is the most important part of any challenge, whether it's one you choose or not. It's how you face this middle part that will make the difference between getting to the top of the mountain or not; finishing the race or not; saying now's the time to end my dysfunctional marriage or not; finding a new job after redundancy or not. All of these moments are going to have a messy bit in the middle.

When we get to the middle we need endurance, energy, passion, the willingness to do the hard work, to be uncomfortable and risk failing.

My focus has been on the excitement of new beginnings and dwelling on the emotional energy of the endings. In every job, every one I've ever had, I've had explosive starts full of productivity, creativity and excitement. But when I get to the middle where endurance is required, I falter a bit.

It's not all it was cracked up to be, yet skipping it would miss all the richness and learning. It is the yukky bit we wish we could skip over. We can't miss this part because it is the most important part of the process. Have you ever set off on a long run and started to doubt yourself halfway through? Started a new job and questioned why you made that decision? Got involved in a relationship and at the point it got tough thought, 'I knew I should have stayed single'?

Yes, not starting is easier and it will never take you to the person you were always meant to be.

How will you keep going through the messy bit in the middle?

How will you stay focused on the end when you still have a way to go?

What if you paused for a minute in the middle and remembered how far you have come?

What if you decided to enjoy the whole adventure, not just the finish line?

14

THE CONFIDENCE MYTH
YOU CHOOSE TO BELIEVE IN GRITTITUDE

No one is normal.

There's no such thing as normal.

We are all unique, complicated, complex, messed up, messy and glorious!

There has never in our history been more discussion and publicity about mental health. We are always hearing about celebrities who share their deep, dark truths, that they too have experienced 'bad' mental health.

What is mental health? What is bad mental health? What, for that matter, is this mythical 'good' mental health?

We have talked a lot already in this book about 'state' and managing your 'state'.

We have already said that happiness is a state. Sadness is a state. Anger is a state. Frustration is a state. Joy is a state.

Experiencing anger, sadness, fear, or anxiety doesn't mean that you have a mental health problem. It just means you have a mind. And remember, you can choose to change your state, and it can take as little as half a second to do it.

Before you take to social media and say that we are suggesting that you can resolve all mental health problems in less than a second, of course sometimes the solution may take longer and may also require outside help, whether that is talking therapy with a coach, friend, or therapist, or whether it is medical intervention. There is a difference between feeling sad and anxious and having a diagnosable mental illness.

It just seems that the media want to turn the experience of every negative emotion into a diagnosis of something that it may not be.

It seems that the majority of people think that if they get sad, or worried, or anxious that they are somehow doing something wrong. That they are suffering from a mental health problem. That they do not seem to be able to be confident, self-assured and resourceful as 'everyone else'. They 'bravely' admit to these negative feelings and think that somehow people will be shocked, surprised or shun them for their failings.

I really believe we have this whole thing back to front.

I am certain that experiencing feeling scared, lonely, nervous, and sad, and thinking that you're not good enough, not thin enough, not clever enough is entirely normal. I am certain that the people who do wake up in the morning feeling powerful, confident, and self-assured are in the minority.

There really is no such thing as confidence, just like there is no such thing as sadness, happiness, joy, or fear.

They are all states. And states are a combination of the stories that we tell ourselves every minute of every day.

What if, instead, we embraced all our amazing states, for exactly what they are? They are reactions to what you are experiencing right now, to the story you are telling yourself.

What if we learned the difference between behaviour and states?

A behaviour is something that you say or do. A state is how you feel.

We can see and hear and experience what someone else says and does but we have to make up the story of how they feel. We don't ever actually know how someone else feels, we just know what they look like they are feeling or what they say or don't say.

What if that person who is smiling, their shoulders relaxed, their hands resting by their sides, is telling you in a slow and articulate manner about their business proposal? Everything you can see and hear is convincing you that they are calm, controlled and confident. They may in fact be feeling terrified inside, and they have just rehearsed and practised until they are able to give a performance that does not give away their true feelings.

What if the person who is fidgeting with their pen, looking down at the floor, talking very quickly and very quietly, and comes across as nervous, is in fact just not very passionate or interested in what they are there to say.

Who do you want to fool, yourself or your audience?

If you want to fool the audience, all you have to do is behave in a way that appears confident even if you are feeling devastatingly nervous on the inside.

Watch people you admire. What do they do, what do they say and how do they say it? Notice how they stand, what they do with their hands, how they make eye contact. *Do they talk loudly or softly, slowly or with energy?* Remember that to fake it you only have to do all the right things on the outside. What is happening on the inside is your own personal secret.

We know you've heard the expression, 'fake it till you make it'. And that's because while you are busy convincing others, your mind is 'listening in' and thinking, 'I'm doing pretty well at this, maybe I am great at it after all.' The more you tell yourself the story of how confident, capable, and brilliant you are, the more you will start to convince yourself and then notice how it impacts your behaviours.

Here are some other tips to help change the story you tell yourself.

Reflect on your achievements

Make a list of all the things you have achieved. Think about work, family, hobbies, and friendships. Think of it as gathering evidence to support the belief that you are a worthwhile person. By bringing to the front of your mind all the positive things in your life, you will have more ammunition when doubt creeps in. You are good enough just the way you are. You just need to remind yourself.

Create a belief wall

Create a compelling visual representation of everything good in your life. Add photos, memorabilia, thank you notes, cards, magazine cuttings, anything that makes you feel positive. Display it somewhere you can look at it when you need a quick reminder of all the good things in your life.

Reframe failure as feedback

If you're afraid of failing, then think of all the opportunities to learn that you are missing. Most learning comes from failing. If you can look for the learning in everything you do, then it will never feel like a failure. Go into new situations with a mindset of curiosity. Challenge yourself to find the learning in every new experience.

Challenge your beliefs

Ask yourself, 'What evidence do I have that this is true?' and, 'What evidence do I have that this is false?'

Say thank you when someone praises you

It can really be as simple as that. When someone praises your work or even simply says, 'I like your necklace,' say, 'Thank you.' You'll immediately feel the lift that the compliment was intended to give you, and you'll make the person giving you the praise feel good too.

Remember, no one else
can see what is going on
inside.
The only person you
have to convince is
yourself.

Sarah's Story

I met Sarah on a leadership programme I was running for a corporate client. After one of the workshops, she asked if we could have some time together to discuss a challenge she was facing. Through the workshop, she realised it was time to do something about it.

We sat down and I asked her to explain what was going on for her.

She said, 'Since I left college a few years ago, I've become more and more anxious in social situations, and now it is creeping into work. I'm always thinking that people are judging me.'

I said, 'Tell me more. When specifically might you feel this way?'

Sarah said, 'I notice it most when I have to present in front of people. I can't sleep for days before. I worry about people thinking I'm an idiot, but I have to do it for my job. I'm so worried that I could lose my job because I can't share the things I need to share with my colleagues.'

I asked if she could think of a situation when she had felt this way before.

Sarah said no. She found it really strange.

I asked Sarah to close her eyes and relax. I guided her through a nice body scan meditation and then asked her again to take her mind back to a time when she has felt like this before. Noticing a shift in her state I asked, 'What has come up for you?'

She replied, 'It's not a time that I've felt this way before. I have been taken back to high school in my mind, to memories of me being mean and judging other people.'

'Okay,' I said, 'so now you are there, what could you learn from this experience? Could you keep these learnings and leave any unhelpful emotions?'

'Yes, I think so,' Sarah said.

'Let's just drop down inside the situation and look at it through your own eyes and see how it feels.'

'I see it differently now,' she said.

Sarah shared that she realised that her being mean to others was at a time when she, herself, had been having a hard time at home. She'd struggled to share her frustration and took it out on some girls at school.

I asked her what she had learned from this new information. After a short reflective pause she replied, 'not everyone is mean and judgemental, and even if someone is, that it's not about me. It's more likely something that's going on for them right now.'

I asked if she could keep these learnings. 'Yes.' She said. 'I'll be more compassionate to others, and knowing this helps me to see others perspectives.'

Sarah called me a few days after this session and said she had just done a stand-up mic night in her home town. She loved it and was looking forward to the next team meeting where she would be presenting.

Even Alice had to fall before she got to Wonderland.

PART 3

DISCOVERING A NEW PATH

How's your ego doing?

We get it, some of the cold, hard truths can be a bitch to hear.

Self-awareness isn't always easy, but we promise it is totally worth it.

By now, some of the mysteries of human behaviour will be becoming clearer. We have cleared part of the path.

We are on this amazing adventure together, yet we don't all experience the journey in the same way. Are you ready to dive in and experiment with some tools, gadgets and magic that will help you navigate the road ahead?

15

THE BROKEN COMPASS

YOU CHOOSE TO BELIEVE THE WORLD IS A THEATRE OF LEARNING

Thomas Edison, when inventing the lightbulb, famously said, 'I have not failed, I've just found ten thousand ways that won't work.'

Why then, decades later, with everything we know about the road to success being paved with lots of failed attempts, do we still fear it so much?

What's so wrong with going off in the wrong direction? Who knows what unexpected surprises you could discover?

How would you experience the world if you never had to fear failure? What if you recognised it as simply an opportunity to learn and grow?

> **What could you achieve if you weren't afraid?**

Ask yourself what failure will look like and what you can learn from the experience of doing it whether the outcome is a success or not. Very often we fear failure even when failure will not mean anything harmful or detrimental will actually happen.

Once again, the shift comes not in the event, but in our perception of it. Choosing to go into a new situation with a mindset of possibility and being open to the opportunity to learn, whatever the outcome, will shift your perception from failure to learning.

Try it out now. *What would you love to do if you were not afraid to try?*

Is it something that could have serious consequences if it went wrong? Is your fear of failure appropriate to the level of risk?

If your dream is to do a parachute jump, then a healthy level of fear is appropriate to make sure that you complete all the checks and take all the safety precautions. If your fear of failure is stopping you from even picking up the phone to talk to someone about how to go about achieving your dream, then maybe your fear is not appropriate at this moment. It is unlikely that anyone in the world has died from sitting on their sofa contemplating making the phone call.

Is fear holding you back?

What would you do if you believed that you could?

Who do you know who has already done it?

What if they felt exactly the same way that you do now?

What would you learn if you failed?

What would you learn about yourself if you gave it your best shot?

> **Be Happy**
> **Be Confident**
> **Be Enough**

16

A 2ND CUP OF TEA

YOU CHOOSE TO BELIEVE IN THE POWER OF BREATH

Jacqui's Story - Breathe

You know those people who get up at five am to meditate while the sun comes up, sipping mint tea, sitting on a cushion, and looking so serene that you want to smack them in the mouth? I'm not a morning person. To be honest, I'm not exactly a night owl either, I'm more of a mid-morning to just after dinner person.

I had this idea that if I was going to become the person I thought I wanted to be, it was definitely going to start with morning meditation.

I just couldn't do it. When I wake up, all I want is a cup of tea and to stay right there in my bed for at least another half an hour while I come to terms with the beginning of the day.

Next, I bring to mind what sort of day today is going to be. I don't have much of a routine, so no two days are ever the same. Sometimes my diary is gloriously empty: no appointments, no commitments; heaven. Other days are packed full of work, volunteering, life admin, or social events. The sort of day that I also love. And yet it takes me a few more minutes to get into the right frame of mind for my quiet or busy day.

By this time, I'm up, dressed, and ready to get going. It's also about the time I get my 2nd cup of tea of the day.

I love my 2nd cup of tea. I'm now ready to breathe, think, reflect, and create.

And that is why, when I started my own coaching business, I decided to call it 2nd Cup of Tea.

If you don't make time for yourself, there never will be time. Finding the time that works for you, not when you think it ought to be, is the first step to creating your own space to think and pause and breathe.

How often have you snapped at the kids, sent an email that you knew, with hindsight, was going to piss off your colleague, or just sat down and cried because it all felt like too much?

Here's the thing...

Self-care is absolutely not selfish.

Taking time for yourself may just be the single most important thing you can do for yourself that in turn also helps you to be there for everyone else around you.

It's all about getting some AIR.

Kay's Story – The Flight

I reluctantly sat on an aeroplane when my daughter was just five weeks old. I was nervous. I've never been afraid of flying, but this was the first time I'd travelled with my child, and everything was heightened as a result. As the voice came over the tannoy, I was horrified at what I heard. Even though I'd heard it many times before, it sounded different this time.

'Put on your own oxygen mask before helping your children and anyone else.'

Seriously? Is this woman crazy? I most definitely will not be doing that, is what I thought to myself.

I realise that was more than twenty-one years ago. Since then the whole concept of 'putting on your own oxygen mask before helping someone else with theirs' has become a bit of a cliché. But honestly, it was many years later, after seriously hitting burnout, that my mind catapulted itself back to that moment and it clicked. It was wise advice.

How do you care for those around you if you don't take care of yourself? And if you don't, who will?

Take some AIR:

Agree your boundaries with yourself.

Impose them obsessively.

Respect them ruthlessly.

When will you take some time for yourself and where will you do it so you will not be disturbed?

It doesn't need you to have a special meditation room or a spa-like setting, although if you have this that sounds heavenly. All it needs is somewhere where you will not be interrupted for just a few minutes.

And just sit. And breathe.

It took me a long time to understand why meditation is all about focusing on your breath. And it's far less mystical than you may think. Breathing is the one thing that you can only do in the moment.

We spend most of our time with our thoughts in the future or the past. Either planning, worrying, and overthinking about things we have to do later today, next week, next month, next year, or thinking about things that have already happened, going over past conversations, decisions, successes, and mistakes.

Mindfulness is all about letting go of these thoughts and being present in the moment. So, focusing on our breath makes perfect sense.

You cannot decide to take a few more breaths today in case you don't have time to do them tomorrow. You can't look back and say, 'I didn't breathe quite enough yesterday; I'll do a few extra today to make up!' It sounds bonkers, and yet we do it with almost everything else in our lives.

You can only breathe now. So, when you focus on your breath, you are focusing on now.

Try it right now for just a couple of minutes. Close the book, close your eyes, and for the next few minutes, just breathe.

How are you feeling now?

If you feel serene and relaxed that probably means you have meditated before and found it easy to drop into a meditative state. If you just spent the last two minutes thinking this is dumb, and I must remember to get that birthday card and reply to that email, and did I remember to switch the oven on?... then you are experiencing what most people experience when they first try this, that our brains are just not used to having some quiet time to focus on breath.

In truth we take breathing for granted. You are breathing all the time, and it just happens without having to consciously think about it so, of course it's getting placed at the bottom of the priority list. If the cars running, why fix it, right? But what if I said you could breathe better, for longer?

In the oldest yogic tradition Vedic Yoga, it is believed that we have a set number of breaths for our life time. Whether that's true or untrue, I don't honestly know, but I do choose to believe it because it motivates me to be mindful of not wasting them. When you are feeling stressed or panicked you will naturally start to take faster, shorter and sharper breaths. Your nervous system is triggered into a sympathetic state, this is when cortisol is released into your system, locking you into a state of stress and anxiety. When you intentionally slow down your breathing, not only do you take less breaths per minute but you also 'switch off' the nervous system on each slow, controlled, out breath, triggering you into a parasympathetic state. Otherwise known as rest and digest or calm.

When you take some time out to learn how to breathe, it will have a massive impact on how you feel and therefore your ability to relax and enjoy things in the moment. So, let's give that another go.

Try it right now for just a couple of minutes. Close the book, close your eyes, and for the next few minutes, just breathe.

Box Breathing

Get comfortable where you're sitting or laying

Close the book

Close your eyes

Bring all your attention to your breath, the gentle rise and fall of your breath

Breathe in through your nose to the count of four

One, two, three, four

Hold your breath for the count of four

One, two, three, four

Breathe out through your mouth for the count of four

One, two, three, four

Hold at the bottom of that breath for the count of four

One, two, three, four

And repeat three more times

Slowly open your eyes and become aware of your surroundings and then simply notice what you notice.

How are you feeling now?

As with all things, if you want to get better at it then practice. There are hundreds of books and apps out there that will help you to develop this skill. Or you could simply find a version that works for you. I personally find more peace when I look at something restful, like a tree, the sea, or the sky, than when I close my eyes. I like there to be some sound too, either the natural sounds of birds in the garden, or the wind in the trees, or a piece of relaxing music. And sometimes I prefer to do something rather than just sit. Going for a walk, writing in a journal, doing something creative like sewing, crochet, painting, fishing, and colouring, can all create this meditative and restful state.

Ruth's Story

Ruth was forty-eight years old and had been working with me for only a couple of sessions. She was a senior leader in a retail business, and we had mainly been working on her career goals. When she joined the call, she sounded harassed. She was talking very quickly and kept sighing heavily, like she was trying to vent all her frustrations by blowing them away. I asked what was going on.

She said, 'Oh, it's ok, I'm just having a really hard time with my son right now, but that's not for now; what I really want to talk to you about is this issue at work.'

After a few minutes talking about work I said, 'I'm wondering if you would like to talk about what is going on with your son?'

She said she thought these sessions were supposed to be about work. I said life didn't really work like that. She went on to tell me about her son's mental health issues. He was suffering with depression. It had been going on a long time, and he was now in his early twenties.

I asked, 'Sorry if this is hard to hear, but I feel I have to ask: have you ever asked him if he has considered committing suicide?'

I saw her visibly relax and look anxious at the same time. She told me that yes, she had asked him, and I could see it was a huge relief for her to be able to talk about it. We spent the next few minutes talking about what support he had and what she was doing to get him the help he needed.

Then I asked, 'And what about you? Who is supporting you?'

She admitted that she had made a doctor's appointment for herself and had cancelled it because she was just too busy. We talked about the impact this was all having on her and the rest of the family, and how she couldn't be the support she wanted to be if she was not taking care of herself.

At this point, she paused for a long time. I watched her as she closed her eyes and just took a breath. Then she said, 'I'm going to call the doctor today and make the appointment again for myself. I don't see anything changing for my son quickly, so I need to take care of myself too.'

We scheduled our next session, and I reminded her that this was an opportunity for her to bring whatever she wanted to work on. I was here for her, not just her career, for her as a whole person.

When do you feel at your best?

What do you do to give yourself the time you need to reset, restore, and revive?

What ritual can you create that works for you?

I'll put the kettle on.

17

THE SPIRIT LEVEL

YOU CHOOSE TO GET COMFORTABLE WITH FEELING UNCOMFORTABLE

Kay's Story – The Run

One day in 2016, I decided to go for a run. The first few steps were awesome. I felt free. I was supercharged!

That quickly changed. After a couple of minutes, I started to feel slightly lightheaded.

A few strides further a wave of sickness came up from my stomach through my entire body.

After less than a mile I felt like I might just drop dead, right there on the road.

You know the kind of experience I mean, right? Maybe you started a new diet, decided to do a new hobby, had a change of career, or something else completely. Just a few days, maybe even just hours later, you started to experience strange rumblings of emotion in your body, a resistance beyond your strength to fight. It can be so frustrating to experience, especially when you don't know why it's happening.

That day in 2016, I stepped out of my front door with grand plans of becoming a runner. My body had other ideas. Very quickly it started to notice changes in my breathing pattern, and with each stride my heart rate changed. Both my breathing and heart rate ventured wildly outside of their normal range. Each breath became shorter and sharper.

———

These experiences are symptoms of a homeostatic alarm sounding.

In an urgent effort to bring everything back into its 'known' balance, the body doesn't bother offering small signs, primarily because we are really well trained to ignore and override them. Most of us don't listen to our bodies when we are feeling unwell or out of sorts. We ignore it.

So, when we are outside of our 'normal range' our body screams as loudly and urgently as it can, to maintain homeostasis.

 "Urgent! Warning! Stop what you are doing. Stop it immediately, or you're going to die!"

From that experience onwards (on a psychological level at least) you may notice a little pang in your body, and a 'don't do it' voice in your head every time you even think about putting on your running shoes.

What is homeostasis?

It's our tendency to prefer that things stay as they already are. We could call it a leaning towards wanting to maintain a relatively stable way of being. We maintain homeostasis through the mental patterns we create. You read about it earlier – it's about taking the path of least resistance.

Homeostasis is also lifesaving. When you're too hot, it sends signals to your sweat glands to make you sweat and cool you off. When you're too cold, it sends signals to your muscles that make you shiver and create warmth. This too is maintaining homeostasis.

Socially, we maintain a stability through things like conformity. For example, we join and stay within particular groups because we are comforted by the ability to maintain attitudes, beliefs, and behaviours which are congruent with our own. This assures little risk of those attitudes, beliefs, and behaviours being challenged. You read about this in the chapter about crabs.

If anyone does try to enter our bucket there are always the golden buttons...

BLOCK, UNFRIEND, LEAVE GROUP

This is one reason 'groups' work so well: they allow us to maintain homeostasis.

There is a constant tension between homeostasis and change. If we become overloaded with change in a short period of time it can disrupt the internal balance. Too little change can lead to apathy.

We may find ourselves wishing our lives to be predictable, solid and unchanging. There is a critical balance between the two systems, and when we attempt to organise our lives to minimise change, we can massively limit both the possibilities for growth and satisfaction in our lives.

Ignoring the presence of change may give us a temporary sense of stability.

This is an illusion.

> **"Whether we like it or not, change is happening in every moment"**

How do we develop our capacity to be open to the possibilities around us whilst our two systems are constantly being challenged and rebalanced?

First and foremost, it's important that we acknowledge that we are constantly working with the balance between homeostasis and change – that we need both.

Attention response

Think of attention as a highlighter. Imagine a page has highlighted sections. Those sections stand out, causing you to focus your attention on those words. Attention equally involves ignoring all competing stimuli.

Attention allows you to filter out information and perceptions that are not relevant at that moment. Your attentional system allows you to focus on something specific in your environment while tuning out irrelevant details, but it also affects your perception of the stimuli surrounding us.

We could practise attention by noticing any number of things. A very simple and effective tool for training our attention is noticing our breathing. Breathing is never constant. Each breath is different. No breath stays fixed for a moment. Even if we hold our breath, our body changes instant by instant in response to that holding. Focusing our attention on breathing is a practice that's available to us all the time.

As we train our attention, we can turn that curiosity to everything.

Rather than making judgements, we can simply become aware of what life is bringing us on all levels. We can cultivate a grateful awareness of the balance in our lives between homeostasis and change.

Set intentions

Before we do any activity, we form an intention. If we want to go and make a cup of tea, it is our intention to do so that gets us to stand up and walk to the kitchen. In this way, intention brings focus, direction and clarity into the mind. Then we are able to carry out what we wish to do effectively.

When we repeatedly renew our intention, we will find it easier to live out this choice.

Making an intention is like shooting an arrow. Once we have shot the arrow we can sit back and relax, allowing it to find its target.

Visualisation

As crazy as it may sound, what I am about to say is true. Your mind can't tell the difference between a real memory and a vividly imagined visualisation! The visualisation establishes a neural pathway which creates a blueprint to be followed in the actual performance. This neuro pathway can be formed in the same way as it would be formed if you actually did it. I know; crazy, right? You can strengthen this connection even further by increasing the intensity of the visualisation and including feelings. It's the fear of the unknown/unfamiliar that causes the homeostatic alarm to ring in the first place. Creating the pathway before it happens means it already feels familiar to the mind.

Many people use this technique to visualise all the potential scenarios they may face, and then visualise how they respond in every situation. I'm talking gold medal Olympians: if it can work for them, it can work for the rest of us!

Create a few minutes every day to see, hear and feel yourself achieving your goal. This could be whilst you're brushing your teeth, in the shower, walking to school or work. Really allow yourself to positively experience it. Notice the obstacles that you may face and notice all the options you have to respond to those different scenarios – and leave that visualisation in the knowledge that you now have options and choices should they arise.

Needless to say, homeostasis makes it difficult to embrace change. It's a powerful force that often results in us experiencing internal setbacks.

The good news is that if you keep pushing, deploying your grittitude in the face of change, homeostasis will eventually adapt to the new, and create a new internal point of reference.

If you keep showing up, your body will eventually get used to the running, or whatever it is you want to become and even begin to crave it. Being a runner, or an athlete, or a writer, or a business owner will become part of your self-image, and you'll experience resistance if you *don't* do these things.

Your friends will get used to this different version of you. They might even join you on your adventure. So, whenever you make a decision that requires a change, expect homeostasis to pop up and attempt to kick your ass. Know that there will be setbacks and keep pushing on regardless with unwavering commitment.

How will you keep your eyes on the goal?

What is your intention?

When you visualise success what do you see, hear, feel, think?

18

YOU BELIEVE YOU CAN CHOOSE YOUR OWN LIFE STORY

Whatever page you are on, the rest of the pages are still blank. What story would your future self like to read?

Be the creator.

Make it an adventure.

Choose your own life story.

ACKNOWLEDGEMENTS

Kay's Acknowledgements

To Jade – My first born. Thank you for giving my life purpose and meaning. You have taught me what true, unconditional love is. We have grown up and learned together. You have a heart pure as snow, and a mind as strong as steel. I am inspired by you every day. I am so proud to call you my daughter.

To Cameron – Thank you for teaching me to expand my thinking, challenge my fears and live life with courage. You surprise me every day. I am constantly inspired by you. I am so proud to call you my son.

To Stewart – Thank you for being the yin to my yang, my strength when I'm weak, and my cheerleader when I'm strong. For supporting my wild ideas. If I am successful, it's because I stood on the shoulders of a giant – that's you Stewart... you are the giant. I am so proud to call you my husband.

To Aaron, Ashleigh, Jamie and Meg – I feel incredibly lucky to have you all in my life. I am so proud of who you are at your very core. You are the grittiest people I know. I am inspired by each of you every day, all for different reasons yet all because of your ability to overcome obstacles and always find a way.

To Mum and Dad – Thank you for every moment of my upbringing; thank you for my brothers and sisters. Thank you for all the choices you made that led me to be the person I am today. I am forever grateful for all those experiences. I am proud to call you my parents. I love you.

To Jacqui – Meeting you has changed my life. You have opened my eyes to so many new ways of thinking and being. You believed in me unconditionally when I didn't believe in myself. Thank you for being the most wonderful precious, beautiful friend.

To Daryll – Thank you for taking me under your majestic wings! Teaching me a fraction of your wisdom, curiosity, open-minded nature and for being a wonderful friend. Eternally grateful.

You are all my purpose; you are my most treasured relationships: I love you.

To everyone who ever told me I was too young, too female, not able to achieve my dreams because I have children, was too ambitious, too vocal, too unrealistic… thank you for being the fuel to my fire. Now pour some on yours.

Jacqui's Acknowledgements

I hardly know how to thank my co-author and best friend Kay for the impact she has had on my life. Without her, there would be no book, no 2nd Cup of Tea, and I would not be me. I was all set to retire at fifty and have a quiet life when she reminded me how much I love doing what I do. She gave me the courage to start my own business and to write this book together. She inspires me, sometimes exhausts me, and amazes me. I will be grateful to you every day of my life.

I want to thank my husband, Malcolm, for supporting me through all my crazy ideas and dreams. I love you. You make me happy every day.

To my Dad, sadly no longer with us, for teaching me to stand up and speak out for what I believe in. I know he would be proud of what I have achieved.

To my Mum, my friend, for always being there through all the messy bits with her pragmatic, it'll all be all right, attitude. My brother Mike, I feel closer to you than ever before, even though we have very different maps of the world. And to my sister-in-law Claire and my wonderful nieces and nephew, Martha, Madeleine and Jude. I love you all.

To my other best friend, Dee, my fellow introvert. You are always there for me when I need time to regroup and reset. Thank you for all you have done to support me, for being the very first person to read this book, and for finding all the typos! I couldn't have done it without you.

To Catriona, for being the first person to ever say the letters NLP to me, David Shepherd for taking me from NLP novice to Master Practitioner in your entertaining, practical, and unique style, and to Karen Foy and Suzanne Hayes-Jones for your wisdom, support and mentoring to help me become the coach I am today.

Finally, to my BT family: I worked at BT for almost thirty years. The colleagues, clients, leaders, and friends I made there are like family. You have given me opportunities, challenges, and fun. You have given me Grittitude.

Thank you to everyone for the part you have played in my life story.

KAY WOODBURN

Kay Woodburn is an award-winning, high-challenge neuro-linguistic programming mindset coach. She has over twenty years' experience working with competitive athletes, leaders and entrepreneurs to master their mindset.

This unique method is the practice of coding how people organise their thinking, feelings, language and behaviour to produce the results they really want. It's a powerful change methodology to model the behaviour you want, to achieve the results you want.

Kay was born and bred in a small town called Darwen in Lancashire, and is very proud of her home town, a true

Darrener. Kay now lives in Cheshire, where she and her husband Stewart have brought up their two children, Jade and Cameron, who are now young adults.

Kay loves working with new people and helping them discover the secrets of effective human interaction. Her family life, corporate career and passion to help people get grittier, led to the founding of Gritty People in 2013. Over the last ten years the team has grown, and the mission has stayed the same: 'to make the Gritty Mindset accessible to all'. The last decade has allowed thousands of people to have just that through workshops, coaching, podcasts and keynote speeches.

You can contact her at www.grittypeople.com

facebook.com/Grittypeople1
instagram.com/grittypeople
linkedin.com/in/kay-woodburn-230a782a

JACQUI FLAVELL

Jacqui Flavell lives in Peacehaven with her husband Malcolm and three cats, Lola, Matilda and Nina. It is her dream come true to live in a beautiful home with spectacular views of the sea, and to help people create and achieve their dreams.

She is the founder and owner of 2nd Cup of Tea, life coaching to help you find your happy.

She has over twenty-five years' experience in Coaching, Learning and Development. Jacqui has worked with global companies and travelled all over the world creating learning solutions in the areas of Leadership Development, Team Performance, and Creating Coaching Culture.

Jacqui is a Professional Certified Coach (PCC) from the International Coaching Federation (ICF) a Master Practitioner of NLP, Timeline Therapy® Master Practitioner, Master Hypnotist, NLP Master Coach and Mindfulness Association Practitioner.

Jacqui is an active volunteer. She has worked as a Wellbeing Coach with Macmillan and continues to support people living with cancer. She volunteers at Haven's Community Hub, a local charity that supports the community and is on the committee of Peacehaven and District Chamber of Commerce, where she provides training and coaching to local businesses.

You can contact her at www.2ndcupoftea.co.uk

facebook.com/2ndcupoftea
instagram.com/2ndcupoft
linkedin.com/in/jacqui-flavell-5983231

NOTES

1. Grittitude

1. Outliers: The Story of Success is the non-fiction book written by Malcolm Gladwell and published by Little, Brown and Company on November 18 2008
2. Theodore Roosevelt "Citizenship In A Republic", delivered at the Sorbonne, in Paris, France on 23 April 1910

www.ingramcontent.com/pod-product-compliance
Lightning Source LLC
Chambersburg PA
CBHW030331230426
43661CB00032B/1368/J